D0056766

Life in the Word Devotional

by
Joyce Meyer

WARNER
Faith®

New York   Boston   Nashville

Unless otherwise indicated, all Scripture quotations are taken from *The Amplified Bible* (AMP). *The Amplified Bible, Old Testament* copyright © 1965, 1987 by The Zondervan Corporation. *The Amplified New Testament* copyright © 1954, 1958, 1987 by The Lockman Foundation. Used by permission.

Scripture quotations marked NIV are taken from the Holy Bible, New *International Version*®. NIV®. Copyright © 1973, 1978, 1984 by International Bible Society. Used by permission of Zondervan Publishing House. All rights reserved.

Scripture quotations marked MESSAGE are taken from *The Message: New Testament With Psalms and Proverbs* by Eugene H. Peterson. Copyright © 1993, 1994, 1995 by Eugene H. Peterson. NavPress, P. 0. Box 35001, Colorado Springs, Colorado 80935. Used by permission.

Scriptures marked KJV are taken from the King James Version of the Bible.

Warner Books Edition
Copyright © 1998 by Joyce Meyer
Life In The Word, Inc.
P.O. Box 655
Fenton, Missouri 63026
All rights reserved.

Warner Faith

Time Warner Book Group
1271 Avenue of the Americas, New York, NY 10020
Visit our Web site at www.twbookmark.com.

Warner Faith® and the Warner Faith logo are trademarks of Time Warner Book Group, Inc.

Printed in the United States of America

First Warner Faith Edition: October 2002
10 9 8 7 6 5 4 3 2

ISBN: 0-446-53209-6
LCCN: 2002110824

Presented to

_____

By

_____

Date

_____

Occasion

_____

Contents

Marriage and the Family

The Good Life

Introduction

Joyce Meyer's life serves as an example of the magnitude of God's capability to fulfill His plan in our lives no matter how unlikely the possibility may seem. In this book you can learn how to experience the same type of victory in your life that Joyce Meyer has experienced in hers. You will glean from the knowledge she has gained of God and His Word on her God-led journey from "ashes" to "beauty" as you read these devotions covering a wide variety of subjects.

Joyce teaches that progress is made as we consistently keep doing what we know to do in God. By reading and applying one devotion in this book at a time on a regular basis, God will use these scripturally based teachings to show Himself to you. He will show you how much He loves you and wants you to learn how to open yourself up to receive all the blessings He has for you.

God wants you to have the type of life He sent Jesus to provide for those who will believe in Him and receive it. Jesus said, *...I came that they may have and enjoy life, and have it in abundance (to the full, till it overflows) (John 10:10).*

As you spend time with God, you can know that He is working to bring the changes you desire in your life. Begin walking on the path, in the plan, God has for you today!

— The Publisher

God Loves You!

For God so greatly loved and dearly prized the world that He [even] gave up His only begotten (unique) Son, so that whoever believes in (trusts in, clings to, relies on) Him shall not perish (come to destruction, be lost) but have eternal (everlasting) life. — JOHN 3:16

John 3:16 tells us that God so loved the world that He gave His only Son as a sacrifice for it.

God loves you! You are special to Him. God doesn't love you because you are a good person or do everything right. He loves you because He is love. Love is not something God does; it is something He is. It is His nature.

God's love is pure and ever flowing. It cannot be earned or deserved. It must be received by faith.

In Ephesians 3:19 Paul prays that we may come to really know this love. When we do, we are strengthened in our inner man. When we are strengthened inwardly, outward difficulties cannot defeat us.

Unless you have received it yourself, you cannot give love away. Let God love you. Receive His love for you. Bathe in it. Meditate on it. Let it strengthen you. Then give it away.

Say This:

"God loves me. I am special to Him. I receive His everlasting love today and am strengthened in my inner man."

Beauty for Ashes

To appoint unto them that mourn in Zion, to give unto them beauty for ashes.... — ISAIAH 61:3 KJV

Multiplied thousands of people have been hurt severely in their lives. They come from broken relationships or abusive backgrounds that are still producing bad fruit in their personalities.

God wants to send the wind of the Holy Spirit into our lives (Acts 2:1-4), to blow away the ashes that are left from Satan's attempt to destroy us, and to replace those ashes with beauty.

The Lord has taught me that consistently bad fruit comes from a bad root. No matter how much we may try to get rid of the bad fruit, unless the root is dealt with, more bad fruit will crop up somewhere else.

God created us to be loved. *He* wants to love us; He wants us to love *each other,* and He wants us to love and accept *ourselves.* Without this foundation of love and acceptance, there will be no joy and peace.

Some of us need to be transplanted. If we started out in the wrong soil, Jesus will transplant us so that we can get rooted and grounded in His love, as the Bible teaches.

Know that you are valuable, unique, loved, and special. When this is your foundation and your root, you will produce good fruit.

Ask God to give you beauty for ashes.

Say This:

"I was created for love. God loves me and wants me to love Him, love others, and love and accept myself."

Do You Feel Rejected?

All whom My Father gives (entrusts) to Me will come to Me; and the one who comes to Me I will most certainly not cast out [I will never, no never, reject one of them who comes to Me]. — JOHN 6:37

God gave me a word for a meeting I was preparing to lead. It is for anyone who needs to receive it:

"Many of My people are in prison because they won't accept themselves. Many of them are gifted and talented, but they won't express themselves because they fear rejection. They fear man. They fear what people will think.

"I want to love My people, but they hold Me at arm's length and won't let Me really love them

14

because they have been hurt by others. They fear I will reject them, as others have, because of their weaknesses. But I will never reject them.

"*Tell them I love them.*

"Tell them to stop trying so hard to be acceptable to Me and to realize I accept them as they are. Tell them I don't want perfect performance from them. I simply want them to love Me and let Me love them."

God will not reject you because of your weaknesses or mistakes. He desires to heal you from past hurts caused by rejection. He wants you to know He will never reject you.

Pray This:

"Father, I thank You that You love me. I thank You that I am always accepted and never rejected. In Jesus' name, amen."

Love Is...

"A new commandment I give you: Love one another. As I have loved you, so you must love one another."
— JOHN 13:34 NIV

Love is the new commandment Jesus gave under the New Covenant. The love walk is a liberating lifestyle because it sets us free from self.

Love is a sacrifice — it costs. Every time we love someone, it costs us something. Time, talent, money, or pride may be the cost.

Forgiveness is love; it costs pride to forgive. The flesh is basically lazy and passive; it always wants effortless benefits. Love is effort.

There seems to be a lack of joy among God's people; one of the major reasons is that we often become passive, looking for an effortless lifestyle.

Love is involvement. It is impossible to have true relationship without involvement. Involvement requires commitment; commitment requires work; work is effort.

Love is an effort; it is an effort to walk in love.

Love is involvement, not isolation. Love requires reaching out. Love says, "I'm sorry," first and initiates the move that can bring restoration and understanding.

Love involves sacrificial giving. Love doesn't do the right thing to get something; love does the right thing because it is right. Love is healing; love restores.

Say This:

"Love is the new commandment Jesus gave. I walk in love, and it sets me free from self. Forgiveness is love, so I forgive."

Living Beyond the Veil

Having therefore, brethren, boldness to enter into the holiest by the blood of Jesus, by a new and living way, which he hath consecrated for us, through the veil....
— HEBREWS 10:19,20 KJV

We can have a close, intimate relationship with God! To enjoy and be assured of God's presence in our lives, we need to spend time with Him daily, fellowshipping and growing closer in our understanding of Him.

We can do things to help us experience His presence or we can do things to hinder that blessing. For example, if we walk in peace and in the love of God — both receiving His love for us and allowing it to flow to others — we experience His presence more.

The Lord will teach anyone who truly desires to know Him how to know Him better. We should find out what draws us closer to God and do those things.

We can veil or block our awareness of God's presence by following our own fleshly desires and plans without consulting Him and by striving to make ourselves acceptable to Him.

Our striving should be in seeking God, seeking to know Him better, to hear His voice more clearly and to walk in obedience to His instructions.

We can experience His presence or the pressures of the world, His presence or desires of the flesh, His presence or religious bondage due to legalism.

Life beyond the veil is wonderful...enter in!

Pray This:

"Father, I want Your presence in my life. Teach me specific ways to learn to know You better. In Jesus' name, amen."

Seek God

You have said, Seek My face [inquire for and require My presence as your vital need]. My heart says to You, Your face (Your presence), Lord, will I seek, inquire for, and require [of necessity and on the authority of Your Word]. — Psalm 27:8

If we want to truly know the Lord, we need to choose to be where He would be, think what He would think, go where He would go, treat people the way He would treat people.

We must seek after the right thing. We need to take an inventory and be sure we are seeking God and not just the things He can do. We must seek His face, not just His hand!

Have you ever spent a lot of time, energy, prayer, and faith on a project only to discover it was an empty well and you were still just as thirsty as before?

I spent many years as a Christian with one faith project after another I thought would surely be "the thing" that would make me feel fulfilled, happy, and contented. I have finally found the one thing that satisfies my soul — the Lord.

Our quality of life does not consist in what the world has to offer, but in God's presence, in His will, in knowing Him and knowing His ways.

Do This:

Take inventory: Are you seeking God and placing His desires first in every area of your life?

In His Presence Is Fullness of Joy

You will show me the path of life; in Your presence is fullness of joy, at Your right hand there are pleasures forevermore. — PSALM 16:11

There are many wonderful benefits from simply spending time with God. The presence of the Lord is always with us, but we do not always recognize it or take time to be conscious of it.

There seems to be a great lacking of contentment not only in the world but also among God's people. Many people spend their lives chasing things when nothing can keep us satisfied except God Himself.

When people are not satisfied inwardly, they usually look for some outward thing to satisfy their hunger. Often they end up in a fruitless search for that which cannot fill the emptiness within.

We've heard it said, many people spend their lives climbing the ladder of success only to find when they reach the top, their ladder is leaning against the wrong building.

When we keep our priorities straight, we discover that everything we really need in life is found in the Lord.

Seek to dwell in His presence. In Him is the path of life, the fullness of joy, and pleasures forevermore.

Pray This:

"Lord, I seek You because I know that everything I need — healing, strength, comfort — is found in Your presence. In Jesus' name, amen."

Be Still and Know That I Am God

Let be and be still, and know (recognize and understand) that I am God.... — PSALM 46:10

One of the most awesome commands that God gives to man is, **"Be still" (Psalm 46:10).**

Our activity when birthed out of the flesh actually prevents God from showing Himself strong in our lives.

This doesn't mean we are to be passive or lazy. It means we are to do whatever God leads us to do, without running ahead of Him in the energy of the flesh.

We need to be careful to submit our ideas and plans to God, then slow down, and wait. Make sure there is a sense of peace to go along with the plans and ideas. Ask the Lord for His will in your life, then be still and know that He is God.

Learn to trust the Lord without having to know what He is going to do, when He is going to do it, and how He is going to do it. Just let Him do it.

If you will turn your heart toward God in loving trust, He will do what needs to be done.

God gives His highest and best to those whose trust is in Him. Be still and let Him show Himself strong in your life.

Do This:

Be still and know that He is God. Be assured that as long as you trust Him, He will never fail you or disappoint you.

In Christ

And you have been given fullness in Christ, who is the head over every power and authority. — COLOSSIANS 2:10 NIV

One of the most liberating phrases in the entire Bible is "in Christ." Through Him all things were created, through Him they now exist, and through Him they will be completely reconciled to God.

Many believers have an identity crisis. They simply do not know who they are "in Christ."

Everything we are and need is found "in Him." In Him we are redeemed. In Him we are complete. Our wisdom, strength, peace, and hope are in Him. Our everything is in Him!

Jesus was made perfect for us. Our acceptability to God is not based on our performance, but on our faith and trust in Jesus' performance.

A *substitute* is "one that takes the place of another."[1] To *identify* with is to "relate (to)."[2] We need to learn to identify with and relate to the substitutionary work of Jesus on our behalf.

Christ came to open the prison doors and set the captives free. The prison is open! Whom the Son sets free is free indeed.

Learn to enjoy the fullness of life Jesus has provided for you. Begin to confess and believe your place "in Him," and your feelings will catch up later.

Say This:

"Because I am 'in Christ,' I am a new creation. Old things have passed away. All things have become new." (2 Corinthians 5:17.)

Abide in Christ

*If ye abide in me, and my words abide in you,
ye shall ask what ye will, and it shall be done unto you.*
— JOHN 15:7 KJV

There are some outstanding promises made in the Word of God to those who learn to abide "in Christ." When we abide in Him, we are living in Him, dwelling in a place of protection, and can rest — trusting, leaning, and relying on Him and His promises. Christ is our place of rest, our refuge, a place to settle down into, and wait for Him to do what we could never do.

As we abide "in Christ," our will is joined with His. His desires become our desires; our concerns become the same as His. We become like Him as we abide "in Him."

Jesus said, *I am the Vine; you are the branches...* *(John 15:5)*. Think about that image for a moment. How long can a branch survive if it is broken off the vine? Christians who have lost, or don't seem to have much life or spark, need to spend more time abiding in the vine.

I have found that when I start to feel dry, withered up, and just plain thirsty, what I need is to get back in contact with the vine.

The life of abiding is a peaceful, restful, and fruitful life. Enter in — and abide there!

Do This:

Ask the Holy Spirit to get involved in everything you do. He is the Helper, and He is waiting for you to ask.

Legalism or Liberty?

Up to this time you have not asked a [single] thing in My Name [as presenting all that I AM]; but now ask and keep on asking and you will receive, so that your joy (gladness, delight) may be full and complete. — JOHN 16:24

God intended for prayer to bring joy.

Every true believer wants to fellowship with God — to talk to Him and allow Him to get involved in every detail of his life. Multitudes spend their lives thinking that they *have* to pray, and therefore never realize that they *want* to pray.

We human beings were created by God for liberty, not legalism. We are to be led by the Holy Spirit and not by the demands of the Law. If we want joy in prayer, we must be willing to follow the Holy Spirit. He brings variety into our prayer life. We can fellowship with the Lord all day long and offer various petitions to Him as well as thanksgiving and praise.

In my own personal prayer life, some days I intercede; some days I praise and worship; at other times I just sit in the Lord's presence and enjoy being with Him.

Don't put God in a box. He has many ways of leading you if you will permit Him to be the Leader while you become the follower.

Do This:

Fellowship with God right now. Talk to Him and allow Him to get involved in every detail of your life.

Lord, Teach Me To Pray

Then He was praying in a certain place; and when He stopped, one of His disciples said to Him, Lord, teach us to pray.... — LUKE 11:1

If we are going to spend time in prayer, we want to be certain that our time is well spent, that our prayers are effective, and that we are praying prayers God can answer. We also want to enjoy our prayer time.

A successful prayer life is not developed overnight nor can it be copied from someone else. God has a personal plan for each of us. We cannot always do what someone else is doing and expect it to work for us. Our prayer life is progressive. It progresses as we progress, so be patient!

Often our prayers are too vague, meaning they are not clearly expressed. When you pray, be clear with the Lord. Pray boldly, expectantly, specifically. Your heavenly Father loves you, so don't be afraid to be bold in prayer. The writer of Hebrews says that we are to come fearlessly, confidently, and boldly to the throne of grace. (Hebrews 4:16.)

If you need help with your prayer life, be honest with God. Tell Him your needs. He will help you if you ask Him to do so. Begin to say, "Lord, teach me to pray."

Do This:

Your prayer life should be enjoyable, powerful, and effective. If it's not, ask the Lord to teach you how to pray.

One Thing Have I Asked of the Lord

One thing have I asked of the Lord, that will I seek, inquire for, and [insistently] require: that I may dwell in the house of the Lord [in His presence] all the days of my life.... — PSALM 27:4

If you will really study and meditate on this Scripture, comparing your own desires with it, you may find, as I did, that you are seeking many more things than the "one thing" to which the psalmist is referring. Imagine being simple enough to desire and seek after only one thing — that one thing being something as pure and simple as dwelling in God's presence.

There are many things in our life we consider needs that are actually only wants.

Years ago I set myself to seek only the one thing in life that is most needful, the presence of the Lord. It has not been easy, but as a result of seeking that one thing I have experienced more of the things I truly want and need — more joy, greater peace, and increased stability.

In Luke 10:41, 42 NIV, speaking of His presence, Jesus said to Martha, *"You are worried and upset about many things, but only one thing is needed...."* I challenge you to join me and multiplied thousands of others who are hearing the higher call to seek the one thing that is most needful.

Do This:

Seek the Lord for the privilege of being in His presence.

Be Healed in Jesus' Name

...in My name....they will lay their hands on the sick, and they will get well. — MARK 16:17,18

There is abundant power in the name of Jesus, and we have been given the right to use that name.

We should speak the name of Jesus in faith against every kind of sickness, disease, and infirmity that arises. We should remember that the Lord gave it to us so we could walk in victory.

We are to pray in the name of Jesus. Prayer is our request — our petition — and the name of Jesus is what gets God's attention. When we pray in Jesus' name, we are presenting to the Father all that Jesus is and has done.

Sometimes we fall into the trap of just putting up with some physical problem, especially if it has been around a long time. We need to be reminded occasionally that there is healing available for us.

If you are sick, fighting any kind of an illness or disease, I encourage you to exercise your blood-bought right to use the name of Jesus against it. Each time you speak that name in faith, power is released.

Start exercising your right to use the name of Jesus against your problems, and believe they lose a little more of their power against you each time you speak that name.

Pray This:

"Father, I thank You for giving me power for any situation in life through the precious name of Jesus. Amen."

Victory Over Addictions

The Lord God is my Strength, my personal bravery, and my invincible army; He makes my feet like hinds' feet and will make me to walk [not to stand still in terror, but to walk] and make [spiritual] progress upon my high places [of trouble, suffering, or responsibility]! — HABAKKUK 3:19

Do you have any addictions?

An addiction is anything that controls a person — anything he feels he cannot do without to relieve pain. The pain may be physical, mental, or emotional. Often addictive behavior is an attempt to hide from reality — to put off dealing with issues that hurt.

Addictions are not limited to substance abuse. Except for cigarettes, most of my addictions did not fall under the heading of substance abuse. I was addicted to reasoning, worry, judgment, compliments, self-pity, pouting, control, and work.

When I realized I was addicted to these things and determined I was going to break my addictions and discipline myself, everything was great until the pain started. If I had not had the inner strength of the Lord to withstand the pain, I would have once again given in to the addictions — which would have relieved the pain but would have started the cycle all over again.

God does not just want to *give* you strength — He wants to *be* your strength. Let Him help you break your addictions.

Do This:

Make a decision today that you are addicted to Jesus and His precepts — that all other addictions in your life will vanish one by one.

Putting the Past Behind

...forgetting what lies behind and straining forward to what lies ahead. – PHILIPPIANS 3:13

God's mercy is new every morning. (Lamentations 3:22,23 KJV.) Each day we can find a fresh place to begin.

I like the way God has divided up the days and nights. It seems to me that no matter how difficult or challenging a specific day may be, the breaking of dawn brings new hope. God wants us to regularly put the past behind and find a place of "new beginnings."

Perhaps you have been trapped in some sin, and although you have repented, you still feel guilty. You may be assured that sincere repentance brings a fresh, new start. First John 1:9 promises a thorough cleansing if you will freely admit that you have sinned.

Once you understand the great mercy of God and begin receiving it, you are more inclined to give mercy. You may be hurting from an emotional wound. The way to put the past behind is to forgive the person who hurt you. Forgiveness is always involved in putting the past behind.

God has new things on the horizon of your life, but you will never see them if you live in and relive the past. Thinking and talking about the past keeps you trapped in it.

Every day is a new day. Don't waste today by living in yesterday.

Say This:

"Today is a new day with new mercies. I put the past behind me. Yesterday is gone. I will begin afresh today."

A Perfect Heart

You, therefore, must be perfect [growing into complete maturity of godliness in mind and character, having reached the proper height of virtue and integrity], as your heavenly Father is perfect. — MATTHEW 5:48

We are commanded to be perfect, and what God commands, He gives a heart desire to attain. Yet, this desire to be perfect can cause a great deal of frustration.

Perfection is a process that is worked out in our lives as we go from one degree of glory to another. There are degrees of perfection. We can be almost perfect in one area, and very imperfect in others.

When we give our will to God, we have a perfect heart. But even at that point, we still have faults, weaknesses, bad habits, and imperfections.

The Lord accepts us as we are and counts us as perfect while we are on our way toward perfection.

If you have given your will to God, this is step one. You now have a perfect heart, and the process has begun.

You are not alone in your travel from glory to glory. Paul said in Philippians 3:12, 13 that he wanted to be perfect, but that he had not yet arrived. He pressed on to things ahead. He knew if his heart was set in the right direction (if he had a perfect heart), that was all God required.

Say This:

"With God's help, I will keep pressing toward perfection. I am growing in maturity, character, integrity, and godliness."

Kingdom Living

But seek (aim at and strive after) first of all His kingdom and His righteousness (His way of doing and being right), and then all these things taken together will be given you besides. — MATTHEW 6:33

As the children of God, it is our privilege to live in His Kingdom. What is the Kingdom of God?

According to Romans 14:17, the Kingdom of God is righteousness, peace, and joy in the Holy Spirit. We can gain everything in the world, but without righteousness, peace, and joy, we still have nothing!

People without Christ have things, but not all of them are truly satisfied. Satisfaction in the inner man is what the Lord wants to give.

Jesus wants us to know that we are right with God because of what He has done for us. He wants us to have peace and joy in the midst of tribulation. Only He can give us that. Things can never produce lasting joy by themselves.

When things are right on the inside, outward things don't matter as much. When they don't matter as much to us, God can give us more of them. When we keep our eyes on the true Kingdom of God — on Him, His righteousness, His peace, and His joy — the rest will be added to us in abundance.

Learn to really live in the Kingdom of God.

Say This:

"Because I seek God's Kingdom and His righteousness, He adds to me all the things I need to live in His peace and joy."

Rested, Refreshed, Revived, Restored, Refilled

Come to Me, all you who labor and are heavy-laden and overburdened, and I will cause you to rest. [I will ease and relieve and refresh your souls.] — MATTHEW 11:28

When we become so burned out, heavy-laden, and overburdened that we feel we are unable to take it anymore, what are we to do? Jesus said, *Come to Me....* But what are we to do when we come to Him? We are to come to Him to *receive!*

If we ask and ask and keep on asking and never receive, then we become frustrated. Jesus wants us to have joy.

One of the major reasons we do not receive is that what has been provided for us is free, and we keep trying to do something to earn it. Jesus has already paid the price.

The New Covenant is according to grace. It is based on the goodness of God and the work Jesus has already accomplished — not on our merit or works.

To *get* is "to acquire as a result of action or effort."[1] To *receive* is "to acquire or take (something given, offered, or transmitted)...."[2] When we *get* something, we obtain it by struggle or effort. When we *receive* something, we obtain it by acting as a receptacle and taking in what someone else is offering.

Receive what Jesus is pouring out. Come into His presence and drink of His forgiveness, His love, His mercy and grace.

Everything you need is available — start receiving!

Do This:

Enter into God's rest and receive what has already been poured out. You will be rested, refreshed, revived, restored, and refilled.

Understanding Your Emotions

Look carefully then how you walk! Live purposefully and worthily and accurately, not as the unwise and witless, but as wise (sensible, intelligent people). — EPHESIANS 5:15

Emotions, feelings, are a part of the soul, given to us by God. A life without feelings would be extremely dry and boring...and yet, if we allow feelings to control us, they can become dangerous and actually make us quite miserable.

Whatever God gives for our enjoyment, Satan will try to use against us. God gave us feelings to be a blessing to others and the Kingdom, but Satan tries to use them to cause us torment. He wants us to make all our decisions based on feelings, to allow our feelings to rule us.

48

Feelings become dangerous and tormenting when we do not understand that we have a choice of whether to allow them to rule us. How often do we feel that someone has hurt our feelings? We can make the choice whether to be hurt or not.

To walk according to our emotions is to do whatever we want now, whatever feels good to us at the moment. Our future is being affected by the choices we make today.

Make your emotions serve you — don't spend your life serving them. Make a decision today to manage your emotions rather than allowing them to manage you.

Say This:

"I determine to manage my emotions. I will make my emotions serve me. I will not spend my life serving them."

Dying To Live

Then the cares and anxieties of the world and distractions of the age, and the pleasure and delight and false glamour and deceitfulness of riches, and the craving and passionate desire for other things creep in and choke and suffocate the Word, and it becomes fruitless. — MARK 4:19

In order to live the "higher life," we must be willing to die to the "lower life."

One of the major reasons people are not rooted in God's Word is their strong attachment to the world. They want the higher life, but they are not willing to give up the lower life.

There is a life to be lived that is so superior to anything the world has to offer that no comparison can be made, but we must die to self and all its ways and demands in order to attain it. We must die to our own ways of being and doing — the fleshly ways of handling situations. We must also die to our own thoughts and our own idle, willful, and contrary talk. We must learn to live beyond our feelings.

The "bottom line" is that God relentlessly pursues the flesh and is intent on setting us free from its control. We must die to live, but it is a positive thing.

Dare to die in order to live.

Do This:

Choose to die to self and the things of the flesh so that you may live the higher life that God has prepared for you.

Combatting Fear With Prayer

...The earnest (heartfelt, continued) prayer of a righteous man makes tremendous power available [dynamic in its working]. — JAMES 5:16

Fear attacks everyone. It is Satan's way of tormenting us and preventing us from going forward so we cannot enjoy the life Jesus died to give us.

Fears are not realities, they are False Evidence Appearing Real. But if we accept the fears that Satan offers and give voice to them, we open the door for the enemy and close the door to God.

Faith is released through prayer, which makes tremendous power available, dynamic in its working.

Satan seeks to weaken us through fear, but God strengthens us as we fellowship with Him in prayer.

The Bible teaches us to watch and pray. (Matthew 26:41.) I believe the major reference in this passage is to watching ourselves and the attacks that the enemy launches against our minds and emotions. When these attacks are detected, we should pray immediately. We may think the attack will go away but we must remember that it is when we pray that power is released against the enemy — not when we think about praying later.

Pray about everything and fear nothing. I believe you will find this decision to be one that will produce more joy and peace for your everyday living.

When fear knocks at the door, let faith answer.

Do This:

Remember that fear is just False Evidence Appearing Real. When fear knocks on your door, let faith answer.

I Will Not Fear!

For God did not give us a spirit of timidity (of cowardice, of craven and cringing and fawning fear)....
— 2 TIMOTHY 1:7

Fear robs many people of their faith.

Fear of failure, fear of man, and fear of rejection are some of the strongest fears employed by Satan to hinder us from making progress. But no matter what kind of fear the enemy sends against us, the important thing is to overcome it. When we are faced with fear, we must not give in to it. It is imperative to our victory that we determine, "I will not fear!"

The normal reaction to fear is flight. Satan wants us to run; God wants us to stand still and see His deliverance.

Because of fear, many people do not confront issues; they spend their lives running. We must learn to stand our ground and face our fear, secure in the knowledge that we are more than conquerors. (Romans 8:37.)

Fear of failure torments multitudes. We fear what people will think of us if we fail. If we step out and fail, some people may hear about it; but they quickly forget if we forget it and go on. It is better to try something and fail than to try nothing and succeed.

Approach life with boldness. The Spirit of the Lord is in you — so make up your mind not to fear.

Do This:

Face any fears you may have. Determine in your heart that fear will not rule your life. Begin to say, "I will not fear!"

The Spirit of Dread

But without faith it is impossible to please and be satisfactory to Him. For whoever would come near to God must [necessarily] believe that God exists and that He is the rewarder of those who earnestly and diligently seek Him [out]. — HEBREWS 11:6

Dread is a close relative of fear. Both dread and fear loudly and clearly declare that we are not operating in faith, which is the only way to truly please God.

Fear frequently prevents us from going forward and doing what we desire to do. Dread steals the peace and joy of "now" because we have a negative attitude toward what we are going to do even though we don't want to feel that way about it.

Understanding that God always equips us for whatever we need to do will bring deliverance from the spirit of dread. We need not dread hard things, new things, challenging things, or even unpleasant things.

We can face life with a confident attitude, knowing that where God guides, He provides. God gives us grace one day at a time just as He gave the Israelites manna one day at a time.

Every time you realize you are dreading something, make a decision to stop dreading and just believe that you can do whatever you need to do with joy because God is with you.

Say This:

"I refuse to dread. I choose to receive God's grace to help me accomplish all that I need to do today."

The Spirit of Offense

Keep and guard your heart with all vigilance and above all that you guard, for out of it flow the springs of life. — PROVERBS 4:23

The spirit of offense poisons lives and attitudes. According to *Vine's Complete Expository Dictionary of Old and New Testament Words,* the word *offense* is derived from a Greek word *skandalon,* which "originally was 'the name of the part of a trap to which the bait is attached, hence, the trap or snare itself....'"[1] It was the part of the trap that lured or snared an animal.

We easily see that offense is what Satan uses to lure people into full-blown cases of bitterness, resentment, and unforgiveness. Satan uses offense to cause us to stumble and fail to go forward with God.

The temptation to get offended is a trap that should be avoided like the plague. If we would not take poison, we should not take offense. If we would be champions for God we must not be easily offended.

Many people never become what God desires them to be because they get offended. They get bitter. Offense becomes a stumbling block to them, and they never progress beyond that point. They are the loser and the devil is the winner.

No person can do permanent damage to you if you are willing to be mature enough to refuse offense and trust God. This kind of attitude will make you a winner in life.

Say This:

"I will guard against the spirit of offense and will not let it get into my heart or life in any way."

Strife

And the servant of the Lord must not strive....
— 2 Timothy 2:24 kjv

Strife is a thief and a robber which we must learn to recognize and deal with quickly. We must control strife before it controls us.

Strife is defined as "the act or state of fighting or quarreling, especially bitterly....discord."[1] It is bickering, arguing, being involved in a heated disagreement, or shows up as an angry undercurrent. Strife is dangerous. It is a demonic force sent by Satan for the purpose of destruction.

The Bible says to resist the devil at his onset. (1 Peter 5:8,9.) Almost any time someone hurts us, or offends us, anger rises up within us. It is not sin to feel anger. But we must not act out the angry feelings in an ungodly way. We must not hold a grudge or get into bitterness, resentment, or unforgiveness. Ephesians 4:26 says don't let your **wrath,** your anger, **last until the sun goes down.**

A judgmental attitude is an open door for strife. We must remember that **mercy triumphs over judgment (James 2:13** NIV**).** Judgment usually leads to gossip. Gossip begins to spread the strife from person to person. It gets us out of agreement, harmony, and unity. It actually moves us out of the realm of God's blessings.

When the temptation comes to judge others, and then spread our opinion through gossip and back-biting, we should remember this helpful hint: Let the one among us who is without sin cast the first stone. (John 8:7 KJV.)

Remember: God changes things through prayer and faith, not through judgment and gossip.

Do This:

Every once in a while read Romans, chapter 14, just to remind yourself that we all have different ideas, opinions, and ways of doing things.

Be Anxious for Nothing

Casting the whole of your care [all your anxieties, all your worries, all your concerns, once and for all] on Him, for He cares for you affectionately and cares about you watchfully. — 1 PETER 5:7

Have you been worried lately?

Worry torments and is totally useless. In the natural realm there is usually plenty to worry about, but the good news is that we believers do not have to live in the natural realm. We have the privilege of casting all our cares on the Lord.

The word *casting* refers to throwing or hurling.[1] We can throw or hurl our worries on God because

He takes care of us. The seed we sow is our care of ourselves, and the harvest we reap is His care of us.

Our refusal to worry shows that we are trusting God. We may speak words that say we are trusting, but actions do speak louder than words in many instances.

Our heavenly Father has promised to take care of us. God is for us, with us, under us, upholding us, around us, and watching over us. In other words, God has us covered! He is our shield and our buckler, our high tower, our fortress and hiding place, our place of refuge, and our sure foundation.

Be anxious for nothing — you are too smart to spend your life worrying!

Do This:

Make a decision now to cast all your care on the Lord and begin to watch Him take care of you.

Do You Fellowship With Your Problem or With God?

Looking away [from all that will distract] to Jesus, Who is the Leader and the Source of our faith.... — HEBREWS 12:2

Do you fellowship with your problem or with the Lord?

The devil wants us to think about our problem, worry about our problem, talk about and try to reason out our problem. God desires for us to spend time with Him, talk to Him, and think about Him and His Word.

Jesus is the One we are to look to in order to have our needs met. If we dwell in Him, our problem has no power over us, but if we dwell on the problem, we magnify it above Him. The more attention we give our problem, the more we feed it, the more power it has over us.

I remember when my husband and I were having financial struggles. I would give Dave the bad report, and he would give me the Word, telling me to cast my care on the Lord. He would fellowship with God while I fellowshipped with the problem. The more I did so, the more upset I became.

The devil starts the problem rolling. The more you think, worry, reason, talk, plan, and scheme about it, the bigger it gets. If you look to Jesus, you will experience the miracle power of God as you trust in Him.

Do This:

Forget your problems. Don't think about them, worry about them, or talk about them. Fellowship with God instead, and you will enjoy life tremendously.

Does Stress Have You Tied in Knots?

...In the world you have tribulation and trials and distress and frustration; but be of good cheer [take courage; be confident, certain, undaunted]! For I have overcome the world. [I have deprived it of power to harm you and have conquered it for you.] — JOHN 16:33

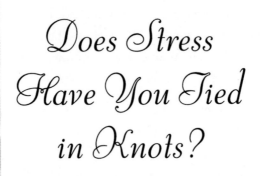

Stress is on the rise in today's world. The good news is that, although we Christians may be in the world, we are not of the world. (John 17:11,14.) We do not have to operate on the world's system — thinking, talking, or acting like the world — and we shouldn't. In fact, our attitude and approach toward the situations of life should be entirely different from the world's.

The source of our stress is not really difficulties, circumstances, and situations, but our attitude and approach toward them.

Jesus said that difficulties will come our way, but they do not have to upset us. We don't have to accept the stress being offered us. We have the privilege of approaching the challenges of everyday life in a calm, peaceful manner.

I believe we can live stress free in a stressful world, but it will require some decisions — possibly some radical decisions.

Allow God's Spirit to lead you out of a stressful lifestyle into one of peace and joy. Change your attitude and approach, and God will change your circumstance in due time.

Say This:

"I choose to receive God's grace today to help me live stress free even in the midst of a stressful world."

What Does Guilt Accomplish?

Therefore, [there is] now no condemnation (no adjudging guilty of wrong) for those who are in Christ Jesus, who live [and] walk not after the dictates of the flesh, but after the dictates of the Spirit. — ROMANS 8:1

Guilt and condemnation are major problems for many believers.

It is Satan's greatest delight to make us feel bad about ourselves. He never tells us how far we have come, but rather, he constantly reminds us of how far we still have to go.

When the enemy attacks me, I say, "I'm not where I need to be, but thank God I'm not where I used to be. I'm okay, and I'm on my way."

Like David, we must learn to keep ourselves encouraged in the Lord. (1 Samuel 30:6.) None of us has arrived at the state of perfection. We cannot perfect ourselves: sanctification (holiness) is the job of the Holy Spirit, and it is worked out in our lives as a process.

The Bible teaches that we can have complete forgiveness of our sins (total freedom from condemnation) through the blood of Jesus Christ. We must decide if Jesus did a complete job or if He didn't. We don't need to add our guilt to His sacrifice. He is more than enough.

Let Jesus do His job. He wants to forgive you. All you have to do is receive His forgiveness. Complete forgiveness is completely free!

Say This:

"I'm not where I need to be, but thank God I'm not where I used to be. I'm okay, and I'm on my way."

Encouragement for the Lonely

...God assured us, "I'll never let you down, never walk off and leave you...." — HEBREWS 13:5 MESSAGE

Many people are lonely, often even those who have others around them. The death of a loved one can leave a person lonely and confused as well as feeling abandoned.

Your circumstances do not have to be quite so severe to put you into the category of loneliness. Perhaps you have moved to a new neighborhood, have begun attending a new school, or have just started a new job, and you just don't seem to fit in yet.

I know what it is like to be lonely. "Social poverty" is under the curse. Learning to like myself and learning to pray for favor have changed my social status, and it will change yours too.

I encourage you to pray for favor. I also encourage you to be friendly. Don't just wait for someone to fall into your life before you are willing to have fellowship. Beware of being passive. Get involved. Giving always brings joy.

Remember Jesus as He prayed in the garden of Gethsemane. All of His friends had disappointed Him. He needed them for only one hour, and they had let Him down by falling asleep. (Matthew 26:36-43.)

The Lord does indeed know how you feel, and He has promised never to leave you nor forsake you (Hebrews 13:5), so that you will be strengthened to press on.

Do This:

If you are lonely, begin to reach out to others. As you reach out, you are sowing seed for your own loneliness to be overcome.

What Should I Do When I Am Hurting?

...forgive....in order that Satan might not outwit us. For we are not unaware of his schemes. — 2 CORINTHIANS 2:10,11 NIV

Most people know what it is like to hurt emotionally. Emotional wounding comes through various sources. Satan is the originator of our wounds, and he works through situations and people to hurt us for two major reasons.

First, he enjoys destruction. He wants to build a dam in our lives that consists of emotional wounds.

Second, he wants to control our feelings. The devil knows that when we have been hurt emotionally, we usually act emotionally. If he can hurt our feelings and get us to react accordingly, he will be able to keep us separated from many of God's blessings.

We cannot expect never to get hurt. But we can expect to learn how to stay in control of our reaction to our hurts. We can expect to be the victor, not the victim.

Here are some things God has shown me we should do to overcome the devil's schemes:

First, turn to the Holy Spirit, don't run to people. Second, remain stable during hard times. Third, remember that God is our vindicator; He will see that we are repaid for our pain and loss.

If you are hurting, I exhort you, don't fall into Satan's trap: be the victor, not the victim.

Pray This:

"Father, whenever I am hurting, I will run to You. You are the only One Who can comfort me. In Jesus' name, amen."

Managing Your Emotions

Be well balanced (temperate, sober of mind)....
rooted, established, strong, immovable, and deter-
mined.... — 1 PETER 5:8,9

An emotional person is someone who is easily
affected with or stirred by emotions. Their conduct is
ruled by emotion rather than reason. A person who
lives by emotion lives without principle.

We all have emotions, and they are not going
away, but we cannot trust them. We should seek God
to learn to manage our emotions and not allow them
to manage us.

We are created to operate in the fruit of self-
control. Self-control is a freedom — not a bondage.
We are free to use wisdom, free to obey God, free to

follow the leading of the Holy Spirit. We are free not to be pushed around by our feelings. We don't have to do what we feel like doing; we are free to do what we know is wise.

Be honest with yourself in this area. If you believe you are not managing your emotions, begin to pray and seek God about emotional maturity. Remember:

1. He who lives by emotions lives without principle.
2. We all have emotions, but we cannot trust them.
3. We cannot be spiritual (walk in the Spirit) and be led by emotions.
4. Emotions won't go away, but we can learn to manage them.

Make emotional maturity a priority goal in your life.

Say This:

"I am well-balanced, temperate, and sober of mind. I am rooted, established, strong, immovable, and determined. I am emotionally mature."

The Inner Life

Cultivate inner beauty, the gentle, gracious kind that God delights in. — 1 PETER 3:4 MESSAGE

We have an outer life and an inner life. The outer life is our reputation with people. The inner life is our reputation with God.

We need to pay attention to what is going on inside us. Thoughts and inner attitudes, motives, and desires — all of these things are important to the Lord.

As far as God is concerned, the inner person is the real person. A truly powerful Christian is one with a pure heart, one who wholeheartedly serves God.

Our inner life is comprised of our soul and our spirit. Our human spirit is indwelt by the Holy Spirit at the time of the New Birth. God's will and desire for us, then, is that we desire and allow the Holy Spirit to dwell in our soul also.

Our soul is our mind, our will, and our emotions. Our spirit mingled with the Holy Spirit performs the functions of conscience, intuition, and communion with God.

We must cooperate with God to allow the divine life force that came into our spirit when we were saved to dwell in and be at home in our entire inner being.

May you be challenged to be accountable for your inner life.

Pray This:

"Lord, I allow You to make Your home in my entire inner being — my soul, as well as my spirit. In Jesus' name, amen."

You Are Private Property — Reserved for God Alone!

[Inasmuch as we] refute arguments and theories and reasonings and every proud and lofty thing that sets itself up against the [true] knowledge of God; and we lead every thought and purpose away captive into the obedience of Christ.... — 2 CORINTHIANS 10:5

If we are going to give God glory, we must manifest excellence. An excellent life begins with an excellent thought life and excellent attitudes.

All fruit has a root from which it began. The root of all of our actions is our thoughts. Words come from thoughts. Attitudes begin with thoughts, and emotions (moods) take root in our thought life.

Choosing excellence in one's thought life is a private thing. No one but God and the individual knows exactly what is going on in his own mind. I call it "inner purity." Inner purity is a challenge that Christians should be excited about taking on.

In Second Corinthians 10:5 the apostle Paul teaches us to cast down all wrong thoughts that disagree with God's Word. He is, in essence, saying, "Keep your minds reserved for God's thoughts (His Word) alone."

God desires truth in the inward parts. (Psalm 51:6.) I encourage you to begin paying more attention to your thought life. Your words, moods, and attitudes are rooted in it. Dedicate your entire self to God. Live as if you were private property — *reserved for God alone!*

Say This:

"With God's help, I determine and purpose in my heart to maintain a godly attitude and to speak only godly words."

When Is Your Mind Normal?

...be transformed (changed) by the [entire] renewal of your mind [by its new ideals and its new attitude]....
— ROMANS 12:2

Every change in our life requires a change in our thinking. God regularly teaches us new ways to think, because we cannot act differently if we don't think differently.

What would be considered a normal mind for a Christian? Remember, what is normal to the world is not acceptable for God's children in most areas. For a believer, worry is not normal. Confusion is not normal.

Negative thinking is another type of thinking in which a Christian should not indulge. There are many other kinds of thinking that should be considered abnormal for a child of God.

The Lord has shown me that when we think hateful, mean, judgmental thoughts about people, not only can we injure them, but also judgmental, resentful, unforgiving thought patterns can cause us great harm.

We have an opportunity to think creative, loving thoughts about people and to pray positive, faith-filled prayers.

Use your thought life wisely. Think about other people the way Jesus would, and think about your circumstances in light of God, Who says, **Behold, I am the Lord...; is there anything too hard for Me?** (Jeremiah 32:27).

Pray This:

"Father, I ask You to teach me new ways to think. Help me to think creative, loving thoughts about others. In Jesus' name, amen."

"Me-Minded"

...If anyone intends to come after Me, let him deny himself [forget, ignore, disown, and lose sight of himself and his own interests].... — MARK 8:34

Having self on the mind all the time insures a miserable life.

I find it a challenge to keep myself off my mind, but the more I obey the Lord's command in this area, the happier I become.

I think all of us form the habit of trying to take care of ourselves. We want to make plans for ourselves and be sure that we are well provided for.

Obviously, one cannot live without giving some thought to himself and making plans, but when you and I move into a selfish, self-centered mind-set, we are out of God's will.

Our society promotes "me-ism," but the Word of God does not.

It is imperative that God's children resist the magnetic pull of worldly ways and refuse to be excessive in self-centered thinking. I believe many people are depressed because they spend all their time trying to make themselves happy. True joy comes only from giving life away — not from striving to keep it.

Don't ruin your life by trying to keep it. Be a blessing to others, and you will be blessed. Give and it shall be given unto you. Die to self-centeredness and really begin to live!

Pray This:

"Father, I ask You to deliver me from self-centeredness and transform me into the image of Jesus Christ. In Jesus' name, amen."

The Wandering, Wondering Mind

Casting down imaginations, and every high thing that exalteth itself against the knowledge of God, and bringing into captivity every thought to the obedience of Christ. — 2 CORINTHIANS 10:5 KJV

Do you ever have any difficulty with wandering thoughts? The harnessing of the human mind is often like trying to train a wild animal. Don't be discouraged. With enough diligence and lots of grace from God, you can win control of your mind.

The key to casting down thoughts and not allowing them to return is to replace wrong thinking with right thinking. Fix your mind on good things. (Philippians 4:8.) Start to think good thoughts on purpose, and you will train yourself to think God-like thoughts.

Wondering about things by turning them over and over in our minds without being able to arrive at a solution leads us into confusion. The Holy Spirit quickened to me that I cannot get confused unless I am trying to figure out something that I need to leave in God's capable hands.

Negative thinking leads to trouble. Proverbs 23:7 says that as a person thinks in his heart, so is he. I believe our thoughts draw a border for our life, and we must live within that border.

Do This:

Choose your thoughts carefully. Meditate only on good (positive) things. Don't allow your mind to become preoccupied with wandering, wondering thoughts, or being negative.

The Search for Peace

...Let him search for peace...and seek it eagerly. [Do not merely desire peaceful relations with God, with your fellowmen, and with yourself, but pursue, go after them!]
— 1 PETER 3:11

When Jesus said, **Peace I leave with you...** *(John 14:27)*, He was talking about a special kind of peace, not a worldly kind of peace. The special peace that Jesus was talking about is the kind of peace that operates all the time in every situation.

The believer who is experiencing God's peace through his relationship with Jesus can have peace even in the midst of the storms of life.

First Peter 3:11 says that we are to search for peace, to pursue it, and to seek it eagerly. The word *seek* means "...strive after, endeavor...desire." "Inquire." "To require or demand."[1] It means requiring something as a vital necessity, craving, or pursuing something.

This verse mentions three areas in which we are to seek peace: (1) with God, (2) with our fellowmen, and (3) with ourselves.

Learn to love peace and to desire it earnestly. Seek peace, for without it you cannot enjoy life and the blessings of God. The Lord has said that if you seek Him with your whole heart, you will find Him. (Jeremiah 29:13.) I believe if you seek and search for peace with your whole heart, you will find what you are looking for.

Say This:

"I have the peace that passes all understanding. I have the peace that operates in the midst of the storm."

The Price of Peace

Peace I leave with you; My [own] peace I now give and bequeath to you. Not as the world gives do I give to you. Do not let your hearts be troubled, neither let them be afraid. [Stop allowing yourselves to be agitated and disturbed; and do not permit yourselves to be fearful and intimidated and cowardly and unsettled.] — JOHN 14:27

The peace of the Lord is one of the most precious blessings in life.

From a spiritual position, it was Jesus' blood that bought our peace. But from a practical or natural position, the price we must pay for peace is a willingness to change our approach to life. We will never enjoy peace without a willingness to adjust and adapt ourselves.

You and I must be willing to sacrifice worry and reasoning if we are to know peace. We cannot have anxiety, frustration, or rigid, legalistic attitudes and enjoy the peace of God.

Keep your mind and conversation on Jesus — not the problem. Worry is useless, vain, and prideful.

One of the big adjustments I had to make was to slow down. It is impossible to remain peaceful and hurry. God is not in a hurry.

Be willing and obedient to make the changes the Holy Spirit leads you to make in order to walk in peace. Jesus has provided His peace — enjoy it!

Pray This:

"Lord, I receive Your peace today. I will seek peace, follow after peace, and let peace be the umpire in my life. In Jesus' name, amen."

God Is Seeking the Pure in Heart

Blessed are the pure in heart: for they shall see God.
— MATTHEW 5:8 KJV

Jesus is coming back for a glorious Church, a holy Church without spot, wrinkle, or blemish. (Ephesians 5:27 KJV.) The Lord is seeking people with pure hearts. (John 4:23.) We should desire and work toward purity of heart because it is God's will. (1 John 3:3 KJV.)

Purity of heart is not a natural trait. It is something that must be worked in most of us. Purity and purging go together. (John 15:2 KJV.) Purging is a tedious process because through it worthless things are removed while things of value are retained.

Removing the worthless without harming the valuable requires an expert — and our God is an expert! (Malachi 3:3.) He watches over us, and when impurities are being extracted, He makes sure the valuable things in us are not harmed.

Allowing God to do a deep work requires great commitment. It is not always comfortable to face the kind of truth He desires to bring. But we must realize that the truth will not affect our lives unless we are willing to face it, accept it, and allow it to change us.

Are you willing to pay the price to have purity in your life — purity of motives, thoughts, attitudes, words, and actions?

Remember, the pure in heart will be blessed.

Pray This:

"Father, I submit my life to You. I commit myself to face Your truth and allow it to change me. In Jesus' name, amen."

How To Hear From God

But when He, the Spirit of Truth (the Truth-giving Spirit) comes, He will guide you into all the Truth (the whole, full Truth).... — JOHN 16:13

Divine guidance is God's will for His children.

We must believe that God does desire to speak to us and that we can hear from Him. One of the ministries of the Holy Spirit in our lives is to guide or lead us into God's will for us in each situation.

I don't believe that anyone immediately knows how to be led by the Spirit. We learn in these areas, and it takes teaching, studying, training, exercising, and making a few mistakes.

Making a mistake is not the end of the world; not learning from our mistake is a greater mistake than the original error.

Have a pioneering spirit and be willing to learn. Here are some pointers that will help you:

1. Have regular prayer and fellowship time with God.

2. Be careful what you hear. Create an atmosphere that is conducive to hearing God.

3. Want God's will more than your own.

4. Know that God leads step-by-step. He often does not show you the entire plan at the beginning.

5. Be a thankful person.

6. Be led by peace and wisdom.

The Holy Spirit desires to lead you into God's good plan for your life; He will speak to you, and you can hear Him.

Do This:

Peace is the umpire that decides what is right and wrong. Don't do anything you don't have peace about. Be led by peace.

Seated in Heavenly Places

And hath raised us up together, and made us sit together in heavenly places in Christ Jesus. — EPHESIANS 2:6 KJV

What does it mean to be seated in heavenly places? It means that we are now able to enter into God's rest.

To be seated means to rest. When we sit in a chair, we rest our physical body. To be seated in heavenly places with Christ is to enter an "inner rest." Our spirit and soul can be at rest because of what Christ has done for us, and because of the good plan God has for us.

One definition of *rest* is "to be at peace or ease"; "free from anxiety or distress."[1] Rest is freedom from worry and frustration which develop because of our works in trying to do what only God can do. It is freedom from excessive reasoning, struggle, fear, and inner turmoil.

We are to abide in the Lord. The word *abide* means to "dwell," "to remain in a place."[2] When we abide in Him, we can rest, trust, lean, and rely on Him in this place of protection. The promise of God's peace is not made to those who work and struggle in their own strength but to those who sit, rest, and abide in Christ.

There are those who have learned the blessing of entering God's rest. They are seated with Him, and they have learned to abide in their place.

If you are struggling, take a seat and rest. Your place has been there waiting for you to occupy it all along.

Do This:

You are seated in heavenly places in Christ. Stay in your seat. Stop jumping up every few minutes and getting out of rest!

Birthing Your Dreams and Visions

Where there is no vision, the people perish....
— PROVERBS 29:18 KJV

It is important to have dreams and visions for our lives. We atrophy without something to reach for. God has created us to have goals. We need to look beyond where we are.

Our dreams and visions are simply hope for a better tomorrow. When God plants a seed of something in our heart, at that point it is a possibility, but not a "positively." That seed must be cared for properly.

Quite often the Lord attempts to place something in our heart, and we fail to conceive that He really means what He is saying. We must remember that we cannot get pregnant with a dream or a vision unless we are able to conceive. Practically speaking, that refers to our thoughts.

We must believe a thing to be possible. We must be able to conceive it in our thoughts. If we do get past the conception, there is still the pregnancy to go through. There is much planning and preparation before the birth. Satan does everything he can to get us to abort our dreams and visions.

God has a vision for your life, and He desires to plant it in your heart. Don't have a "spiritual abortion." Give birth to all that God has placed within you.

Say This:

"I will not give up the dreams and visions God has placed within my heart. I am determined to see them through to the end."

The Time Is Now!

The thief comes only in order to steal and kill and destroy. I came that they may have and enjoy life, and have it in abundance (to the full, till it overflows). — JOHN 10:10

We must learn to be "now" people and not relegate everything to the future.

I believe it is time to possess the land, time to get very serious. We need to take a more aggressive stand concerning possessing what Jesus died to give us. We can think about it, dream about it, talk about it, but it is time to actually have and enjoy all that Jesus has in mind for each of us.

The blessings of God don't simply fall on us. We must stand our ground and possess what is rightfully ours. We can easily get the mistaken idea that we are to limp along here on earth while just looking forward to the blessings of heaven later on.

Have an aggressive faith toward the covenant blessings that God has promised. Start confessing that you are blessed and that the good things of God flow to you in abundance.

The Greater One lives in you. You can do whatever you need to do by His power. Believe it! Don't wait to believe it until later on, but do it now.

Make a decision to be a "now" person.

Say This:

"I believe now, I obey now, I give now, I pray now. I am possessing the land — *not later, but now!*"

The Power of Weakness

For we do not have a High Priest Who is unable to understand and sympathize and have a shared feeling with our weaknesses and infirmities and liability to the assaults of temptation, but One Who has been tempted in every respect as we are, yet without sinning.

Let us then fearlessly and confidently and boldly draw near to the throne of grace (the throne of God's unmerited favor to us sinners), that we may receive mercy [for our failures] and find grace to help in good time for every need [appropriate help and well-timed help, coming just when we need it]. — HEBREWS 4:15,16

The only power that weakness has over us is the power we give it by fearing it. God promises to strengthen us in our weaknesses if we trust Him and turn to Him. (Isaiah 41:10.) We must have faith concerning weaknesses and not fear them. God's grace will be sufficient in our need. (2 Corinthians 12:9.)

We can come to Jesus just as we are. He takes us "as is" and makes us what we ought to be.

Our weaknesses are a greater problem for us than for God. He understands them and is willing to give us grace. We receive grace through the channel of faith.

I encourage you to start receiving and stop grieving over your weaknesses. It is time to go forward.

Pray This:

"Father, thank You for strengthening me in my weaknesses. I believe Your grace is sufficient for every situation I face. In Jesus' name, amen."

In God's Waiting Room

My times are in Your hands.... — PSALM 31:15

If we could understand God's timing, we could better cooperate with His plan for our lives. However, we may never completely understand. When we don't know, we must be satisfied to know the One Who knows. If we are going to walk with Him and enjoy His blessings, we must learn to let God be God.

Most of us attempt to take the lead role in our relationship with the Lord. He has a position, and He will not change it. We must change. He has the lead role. He gives the instructions, and we follow — even though we don't always like the way He chooses to take us.

Timing is an important issue in our walk with God. Why does it take God so long to do what we ask Him to do? Trust always requires unanswered questions which keep us growing in faith.

God has a plan and a timing. While we are in God's waiting room, He is getting us ready for what He already has prepared for us. We must grow up and mature. It takes time. As we reach new levels of maturity, God releases new levels of blessings.

You may be in the habit of taking care of yourself. Retire from self-care. God wants to take care of you. He is faithful, and you can depend on Him.

Pray This:

"I trust You, Lord. I know that You love me and that Your plan and timing for me are perfect. In Jesus' name, amen."

Let God Be God — of the Present

Some trust in and boast of chariots and some of horses, but we will trust in and boast of the name of the Lord our God. — PSALM 20:7

There are many facets of faith. The most brilliant facet, however, is trust!

Trust is something we have, and we decide what to do with it. We decide in whom or in what to put our trust.

We must remember Who delivered us in the past and know Who will deliver us in current troubles, then take our trust and put it in the right place, which is in God alone.

Trust has certain identifying characters. Trust is not upset, because it has entered into God's rest. Trust is not confused, because it has no need to lean to its own understanding. Trust does not indulge in carnal reasoning, it lets God be God.

In whom have you placed your trust? In what have you placed your trust? Is your trust in your job, employer, bank account, natural talents, or friends?

Perhaps your trust is in yourself, your past record of successes, education, or possessions. All of these things are temporal. They are subject to change. Only the Lord changes not. He alone is the Rock that cannot be moved.

Choose to place your trust in God. It requires a greater faith, but it pays outstanding dividends.

Say This:

"I trust in the Lord with all of my heart and mind. I will not rely on my own insight or understanding."

Grace, Grace, and More Grace

But He gives us more and more grace (power of the Holy Spirit, to meet this evil tendency and all others fully)....God sets Himself against the proud...but gives grace [continually] to the lowly (those who are humble enough to receive it). — JAMES 4:6

All human beings have evil tendencies, but James teaches us that God will give us more and more grace to meet these tendencies.

I spent much of my Christian life trying to meet my own evil tendencies. All my trying brought much frustration. I had to come to a place of humility. I had to learn that God gives grace to the humble — not the proud.

We have our own ideas about what we can accomplish, but often we think more highly of ourselves than we ought. We should have a humble attitude, knowing that apart from God, we can do nothing.

If you are planning your own way, trying to make things happen in the strength of your own flesh, then you are frustrated. You probably have said, "No matter what I do, nothing seems to work!" Nothing will ever work until you learn to trust in God's grace.

Relax. Let God be God. Stop being so hard on yourself. Change is a process, it comes little by little.

You are on your way to perfection. Enjoy the trip!

Pray This:

"Father, I receive Your grace today. I receive the power of the Holy Spirit to meet my evil tendencies. In Jesus' name, amen."

No Flesh Shall Glory

And God also selected (deliberately chose) what in the world is lowborn and insignificant and branded and treated with contempt, even the things that are nothing, that He might depose and bring to nothing the things that are, so that no mortal man should [have pretense for glorying and] boast in the presence of God. — 1 Corinthians 1:28,29

It remains to be seen what God can do through a man or woman who will give Him all the glory.

God often chooses unlikely people through whom to work. He does so because there is a better chance that He will get the glory if He uses people who are nothing and have nothing going for them in the natural.

All good does issue from God, and in us (in our flesh) there is no good thing. Whatever good that does occur through us is a manifestation of God flowing through us and should provoke in us a thankful heart that God has chosen to use us.

We should not be looking for human honor or mortal fame, but rather, we should be seeking God's approval. If we will live our lives to glorify God and not seek glory for ourselves, He will take care of making sure that we are blessed and honored.

Seek to be well-known in the spiritual Kingdom — not necessarily among men.

Do This:

If you believe you are called by God, seek humility. God will see to your fame in His timing and in His own way.

What Is God Doing in My Life?

Lean on, trust in, and be confident in the Lord with all your heart and mind and do not rely on your own insight or understanding. — PROVERBS 3:5

Do you find yourself saying, "God, what are You doing in my life?"

Confusion occurs when we try to figure out what we do not understand. As believers, we have a unique privilege, which is to remain in peace even when we do not understand what has happened, what is happening, or what is going to happen in the future. We can be content to know the One Who knows, even if we do not know the answer ourselves.

We serve the All-Knowing God Who keeps one eye on us all the time. God is never surprised; He knows everything before it happens.

We should grow in trust not questions. We are generally more concerned with temporal things, and God is concerned with eternal things. Something may be God's will for us, but not His perfect timing. We must learn to wait on Him.

I had to learn early to lean on, trust in, and be confident in the Lord. Through experience, I have learned to say, "God, I do not know what You are doing, but I am sure You do. I trust You."

Trust God and by doing so you will maintain your peace.

Say This:

"God has a good plan for my life. I choose to trust and wait on Him even when I don't understand what He is doing."

Casting All Your Cares

Therefore humble yourselves...casting the whole of your care [all your anxieties, all your worries, all your concerns, once and for all] on Him, for He cares for you affectionately and cares about you watchfully. — 1 PETER 5:6,7

Worry, anxiety, and care have no positive effect on our lives. They do not bring a solution to problems. They do not help us achieve good health, and they prevent our growth in the Word of God.

One of the ways that Satan steals the Word of God from our heart is through cares. The Bible says we are to cast our cares onto God, which is done by prayer. We cannot handle our own problems; we are not built for it. We are created by God to be dependent upon

Him, to bring Him our challenges and to allow Him to help us with them.

We must not take the care upon ourselves. Keeping our cares is a manifestation of pride. It shows that we think we can solve our own problems and that we don't need the Lord.

We show our humility by leaning on God. Worry, anxiety, and care are not manifestations of leaning on God, but they clearly state by their mere existence that we are attempting to take care of ourselves.

Pray about everything and worry about nothing. You will enjoy life much more.

Pray This:

"Father, show me each time I take a care instead of casting it. Then I will immediately cast it on You. In Jesus' name, amen."

How To Be Content

...I have learned how to be content (satisfied to the point where I am not disturbed or disquieted) in whatever state I am. — PHILIPPIANS 4:11

The Bible teaches us to be content no matter what our circumstances may be. (Hebrews 13:5 KJV.)

We are not to be upset about anything, no matter what is happening. Instead we are to pray about it, and tell God our need. While we are waiting for Him to move, we are to be thankful for all that God has done for us already. (Philippians 4:6.)

I have discovered that the secret of being content is to ask God for what I want, and know that if it is right He will bring it to pass at the right time, and if it is not right, He will do something much better than what I asked for.

We must learn to trust God completely if we ever intend to enjoy peaceful living. We must meditate on what God has done in our life instead of what we are still waiting on Him to do.

God loves you. He is a good God Who only does good things. Be content knowing that His way is perfect, and He brings with Him a great recompense of reward for those who trust in Him. (Hebrews 10:35 KJV.)

Trust God. Hide yourself in the secret place (in Him).

Pray This:

"Lord, I choose to trust You completely. Whatever the situation, I make the decision to be peaceful and content. In Jesus' name, amen."

Let God Be God — of the Future

For I know the thoughts and plans that I have for you, says the Lord, thoughts and plans for welfare and peace and not for evil, to give you hope in your final outcome. — JEREMIAH 29:11

God has a plan and a purpose for each of us and a specific way and perfect time to bring it to pass.

Much of our frustration and misery comes from either not believing that fact, or believing it but being determined to do things our own way and in our own time, determined to exalt our own will and timing above God's.

According to Isaiah 55:8, God's thoughts are not our thoughts, and His ways are not our ways. We want what feels good right now, but God has something far greater in mind.

We are constantly trying to figure out something we do not understand or trying to make something happen *now* that is not happening yet. It seems as if we are always trying, but believers are supposed to *believe!*

"Why, God, why?" and "When, God, when?" can be two statements that keep us frustrated and prevent us from enjoying peace. Many times we do not understand what God is doing. But that is what trust is all about. Let God be God in your life. Give Him the reins. He knows what He is doing.

Do This:

Trust yourself and everything to God Who judges fairly and deals righteously. Deposit yourself in His hands and watch what He can do!

The Mercy of God

Blessed (happy, to be envied, and spiritually prosperous — with life-joy and satisfaction in God's favor and salvation, regardless of their outward conditions) are the merciful, for they shall obtain mercy! — MATTHEW 5:7

Mercy appears to be somewhat a matter of sowing and reaping, and I am sure we all want to reap mercy. Therefore, we should learn how to sow it toward a plentiful harvest available when we need it.

What is *mercy*? It is an attribute of God's character that is seen in how He deals with His people. Mercy is good to us when we deserve punishment. Mercy accepts and blesses us when we deserve to be totally rejected. Mercy understands our weaknesses and infirmities and does not judge and criticize us.

I went through a period in my walk with God in which He was trying to teach me the importance of mercy and being merciful. He taught me that I was unable to give mercy to others because I did not know how to receive mercy from Him.

The love of God works the same way. Many are unable to walk in love; one of the reasons is that they have never received the love of God for themselves, so they have none to give away.

Receive God's mercy and love; you cannot give away something you do not have.

Do This:

Begin receiving mercy on a regular basis. As you do, you will find that you have mercy to give to others.

Are You Holding a Grudge — or Is a Grudge Holding You?

...forgiving one another [readily and freely], as God in Christ forgave you. — EPHESIANS 4:32

When we hold things against people, are we really hurting them? Isn't it really ourselves we are hurting?

Jesus frequently spoke of the need to forgive others. If we are to walk the narrow path, we will have to learn to be quick to forgive. The quicker we forgive, the easier it is. We must do it before the problem gets rooted in our emotions. It will be much more difficult to pull out if it has long, strong roots.

Holding grudges against other people does not change them, but it does change us. It makes us sour, bitter, miserable, and difficult to be around. When we think we are holding a grudge, it is actually the grudge that is holding us. It is Satan's deceptive way of keeping us in bondage. He wants us to think we are getting even, that we are protecting ourselves from being hurt again.

None of that is true!

I want to encourage you to ask God for grace to forgive anyone against whom you are holding a grudge. Determine from this point on to keep your heart and life free from this negative emotion.

God has a great plan for your life, but you will only enter into it by staying on the narrow path.

Say This:

"I choose to follow Jesus' example by forgiving others. Therefore, I enter into a new realm of peace and enjoyment of life."

Blessed Are the Merciful

Blessed are the merciful: for they shall obtain mercy.
— MATTHEW 5:7 KJV

Being merciful can be defined as giving good that is undeserved. Anyone can give people what they deserve. It takes someone full of Jesus to give good to people when they do **not** deserve it.

Revenge says, "You mistreated me, so I'm going to mistreat you." Mercy says, "You mistreated me, so I'm going to forgive you, restore you, and treat you as if you never hurt me." What a blessing to be able to give and receive mercy.

To be merciful is to see "the why behind the what." In other words, mercy doesn't just look at what a person does, but seeks to understand why he did what he did.

Being merciful does not mean we don't deal with issues. It means we have a forgiving, understanding attitude while we deal with them.

God is merciful to us, and He is giving us a chance to be blessed by giving mercy to others.

Do you ever need God or man to show you mercy? Of course, we all do on a regular basis. The best way to get mercy is to be busy giving it away.

Give judgment, and you will receive judgment. Give mercy, and you will receive mercy.

Remember, you reap what you sow. Be merciful! Be blessed!

Pray This:

"Father, thank You for Your mercy. I receive it by faith and determine to give it to others. In Jesus' name, amen."

Only Imperfection Is Intolerant of Imperfection!

Not that I have now attained [this ideal], or have already been made perfect, but....I press on toward the goal to win the [supreme and heavenly] prize to which God in Christ Jesus is calling us upward. — PHILIPPIANS 3:12,14

"If there is one mark of perfection, it is simply that it can tolerate the imperfections of others." This statement was made by François Fénelon in the seventeenth century. When I read that statement in a book recently, it gripped my heart, and I knew it was something I needed to meditate on.

The apostle Paul stated that he pressed on toward the mark of perfection. I believe all those who truly love the Lord are compelled to do that. He is perfect, and our journey into Him compels us to be like Him. We want to do things the right way — the way that would be pleasing to Him.

Perhaps a good measuring stick of our perfection is how patient we are with the imperfections of others. When I am impatient with others because of their imperfections, if I take a moment and consider my own imperfections, I usually get patient again very quickly.

If you have an imperfection, don't be down on yourself. God will help you. If you are impatient with the imperfections of others, remember that only imperfection is intolerant of imperfection.

Say This:

"I determine to be tolerant of the imperfection of others, because I realize that I also have imperfections which God is perfecting in me."

The School of Obedience

...I have set before you life and death, the blessings and the curses; therefore choose life, that you and your descendants may live. — DEUTERONOMY 30:19

God has created us with a free will. That means that we have the awesome responsibility of choosing His way or rejecting it.

God loves us more than we can begin to understand. He wants the best for us, but His Word says that He sets before us a choice. He respects our right to choose and will neither manipulate us nor control us.

The Holy Spirit seeks to work in our lives to lead us down the good path God has planned, but if we are rebellious and disobedient and persist in walking our own way, we will be allowed to do so, even though it grieves the heart and Spirit of God.

There are many believers who have never enjoyed the good life God has prearranged for them simply because they have refused to be obedient to Him. Far too many of God's children are not living the abundant life He wills for them because they choose to walk their own way.

You will be faced with many opportunities to obey or disobey. God has promised that if you choose to walk in His will, you will walk in the good life.

Only you can make your decision.

Do This:

Choose to obey God. Choose a lifestyle of obedience, and you will experience the good life that God has planned for you.

Whom Will You Serve?

...If anyone intends to come after Me, let him deny himself [forget, ignore, disown, and lose sight of himself and his own interests] and take up his cross, and...follow with Me [continually, cleaving steadfastly to Me].
— MARK 8:34

Jesus is coming back for a glorious Church without spot, wrinkle, or blemish. (Ephesians 5:27 KJV.) One of the best ways to become glorious quickly is through prompt and extreme obedience.

Obedience and selfishness are opposing forces. If we are to be glorious, we must be obedient. In order to be obedient, we must be willing to say no to self daily. We must learn to say, "Yes, Lord, yes," and to say it quickly!

We need to learn to follow the promptings of the Holy Spirit. He lives in us and is constantly attempting to lead and guide us. He gently lets us know when we are going in the right direction or the wrong direction.

Obedience to the Lord requires developing sensitivity to His ways, which comes through His Word. We are not just to read the Word, but to do the Word. (James 1:22.)

Make a decision today that you are going to come up higher into a new level of obedience. The rewards of an obedient lifestyle are well worth the price.

Choose you this day whom you will serve — the flesh or the Spirit.

Pray This:

"Father, I choose to be obedient in every area of my life. I will follow Your plan and not my own. In Jesus' name, amen."

The Anointing

But it is God Who confirms and makes us steadfast and establishes us [in joint fellowship] with you in Christ, and has consecrated and anointed us [enduing us with the gifts of the Holy Spirit]. — 2 Corinthians 1:21

The anointing is one of the most important things in our life and ministry. It causes us to have supernatural ability and strength. The anointing is God's power — His ability resting on us to help us do things with ease that would otherwise be hard.

I believe one of Satan's greatest tricks is that of getting us to run around trying to get something we already have and to be something we already are!

Every one of us has a purpose — a gifting and a calling — and we don't need to be overly concerned about what it is or compare it with anyone else's.

First John 2:20 tells us that we *have been* anointed — past tense. Once we know we are anointed, we can learn how to release the anointing in us. I believe we experience the anointing as we use our gifts.

God did not share His power with us so we could sit and do nothing with it. We are empowered by the anointing for service. We have a destiny!

You will never be anointed to be anyone else. Be careful of comparison and competition. Just be yourself.

Say This:

"My eyes are on God. I am walking in obedience to Him. Nothing can hold me back. I am anointed for His purpose."

Time Management and Priorities

Look carefully then how you walk! Live purpose-fully and worthily and accurately,...as wise (sensible, intelligent people), making the very most of the time....
— EPHESIANS 5:15,16

We are the generation God has set apart to participate in the end-time harvest that is prophesied in His Word. God is searching for people He can trust to be accountable for the anointing, power, and authority that will be evident in these last days.

Learning to walk in obedience where we are prepares us for the next level into which God wants to take us. Obedience prepares us for promotion. We cannot wait until the "glory days" hit and then get prepared. Preparation precedes promotion.

God is speaking to His people today saying, "Get your house in order." What does this mean in a practical way? I believe it means that we are not to live fragmented, useless lives with no purpose and direction. We must be accountable and responsible for the abilities God has given each of us. We must make a firm decision to stop wasting our time, because time is a gift from God.

Time management is vital to preparation and equipping. Funnel your time into your purpose. Don't look at your time as your own, but see it as God's — something He has entrusted to you to use wisely.

Say This:

"I will no longer procrastinate or be slow of heart to believe. I will move when the Lord says, 'Move!'"

Discipline and Self-Control

For we are...recreated in Christ Jesus, [born anew] that we may do those good works which God predestined...for us...that we should walk in them [living the good life which He prearranged and made ready for us to live]. — EPHESIANS 2:10

Everyone wants the good life; not everyone wants to live a disciplined and self-controlled lifestyle. Without discipline and self-control, we will never enjoy the good life that God has prepared for us.

To live a disciplined life we cannot do what we feel like doing. Discipline and self-control require denial of the flesh, but they lead to the good life, the kind of life in which we find peace, joy, power, and many other good things.

You and I don't have to live a disciplined life. God will still love us with or without discipline on our part. But if we want to live the good life He desires for us, we must choose discipline and self-control. Neither of these things is easy on the flesh, but the victory we enjoy is worth the suffering we must endure to obtain it.

Discipline is a choice, not a law. It is a tool we believers use to lead ourselves into victory.

I exhort you to be a disciplined person who operates in the fruit of self-control.

Do This:

Practice self-control in every area of your life. Discipline the flesh, then enjoy the good life that comes. It's a choice.

Is God Dealing With You?

You must submit to and endure [correction] for discipline; God is dealing with you as with sons. For what son is there whom his father does not [thus] train and correct and discipline? — HEBREWS 12:7

The Bible teaches us about God's chastisement. (Hebrews 12:8 KJV.) The word *chastisement* means correction.[1] Like any good father, God corrects His children because He loves them.

Many people get discouraged when God deals with them. As soon as He shows them their faults, they become anxious, worried, and upset.

We should rejoice when God shows us our faults and cheerfully submit to His correction. We should get in agreement with Him.

The Holy Spirit brings conviction; the devil wants to take the conviction and turn it into condemnation (guilt). God doesn't want us to feel condemned when He shows us our faults. He wants us to agree with Him. He wants us to face truth because it is truth that will set us free. (John 8:32.) When we face truth, God is right there, ready to give us mercy.

When God corrects you, don't come under condemnation. Correction is a fact of life. It is a continuous process that goes on all the time in the life of the believer.

Allow God to have His way in your life. Be glad when He corrects you. The correction is making you better.

Do This:

Rejoice when God corrects you and cheerfully submit to Him. Be quick to get in agreement with Him and quick to change.

Are You Able To Drink the Cup That Jesus Drank?

...Are you able to drink the cup that I am about to drink.... — MATTHEW 20:22

This was Jesus' response to the request of His disciples James and John to sit on His right and left hand.

Many people want God to bless them with a high position, but they are not ready to stop living a self-centered life. God considers selfishness to be a low level of living.

We can choose to spend our lives trying to get what we want when we want it, but it is a lower life.

There is a higher life. If we will not give up the lower life, we will never have the higher life. But if we are willing to give up the lower (natural) life, then God will give us the higher (spiritual) life.

Jesus is now seated at the right hand of the Father. He had to lay down the lower life first before He got the higher life.

In order to be promoted as Jesus was, we must crucify the flesh. We must forget about ourselves — stop thinking about ourselves, talking about ourselves, and trying to get our own way. We must first make an investment, then God will give us a mighty return.

If you want the higher life, be willing to drink the cup that Jesus drank — the cup of unselfishness.

Pray This:

"Father, in the name of Jesus, I break the bondage of selfishness off my life. Thank You that I am free."

Lazy and Lukewarm

...stir up (rekindle the embers of, fan the flame of, and keep burning) the [gracious] gift of God, [the inner fire] that is in you.... — 2 TIMOTHY 1:6

We need to be on our guard against the spirit of passivity. Passivity is one of the greatest tools that Satan uses against God's people. Procrastination and laziness are the cousins of passivity, and they usually all attack in a group. A passive person waits to be moved by an outside force before he will take action. We are to be motivated and led by the Holy Spirit within us, not by outside forces.

In Revelation 3:16 Jesus warns that He will not be satisfied with lukewarmness. We need to be full of the zeal of God.

I don't know about you, but I don't usually wake up in the morning feeling full of zeal. But thank God I have learned how to "stir up the gift within me." I have discovered that the Word of God coming out of my own mouth in prayer, praise, preaching, or confession is the best encouragement I can find. It stirs up the gift within, keeps the fire aflame, and prevents me from becoming lukewarm.

I strongly encourage you to refuse passivity, procrastination, and laziness. Act now with all diligence and zeal according to the Word of God. Stir up the inner flame!

Do This:

Refuse to be passive and lazy. Stir up the gift within you by keeping the Word of God coming out of your mouth!

Anointed To Be Quiet

He who guards his mouth keeps his life, but he who opens wide his lips comes to ruin. — PROVERBS 13:3

Are you anointed to be quiet?

The apostle Paul writes of the dangers of empty, silly, useless talk. (Ephesians 5:4; 1 Timothy 6:20; 2 Timothy 2:16.) The writer of Proverbs warns that a man who rashly speaks out everything that passes through his mind will end up in disaster.

There was a time in my life when I just could not keep quiet. I have always been a talker, and that is not all bad if a person can learn wisdom concerning timing. I have learned how to be quiet to go along with my God-given ability to speak and communicate.

142

Balance is the key to staying out of trouble.

Perhaps you are a talker, and you have not yet allowed God to anoint you to be quiet. Let me remind you that James says no man can tame the tongue. (James 3:8.) You will definitely need God's help. Ask the Lord to quicken you each time you are talking too much or too loudly, or when it is simply not necessary.

Remember to think before you speak. James says to be quick to hear, slow to speak, and slow to anger. (James 1:19.)

I ask again, are you anointed to be quiet? If not, ask God to help you.

Pray This:

"Father, quicken me when I am talking too much or too loudly and teach me when to be quiet. In Jesus' name, amen."

Finding and Fulfilling Your Destiny

For a wide door of opportunity for effectual [service] has opened to me [there, a great and promising one], and [there are] many adversaries. — 1 CORINTHIANS 16:9

God promotes us into the fullness of His will in degrees or stages. Satan opposes each new phase of our progress. If we do not understand this fact we will become confused and think we have made a mistake.

Satan seeks to wear us out. He wants to bring such opposition against us that we become so weary and discouraged we give up. With opportunity comes opposition.

We must beware of compromise. Satan doesn't want us in the will of God, fulfilling our destiny. If he cannot keep us completely out of God's will, his next tactic is to tempt us to do a little less than what God has said.

Satan tempts us to compromise. But he fails to tell us that in the end we will feel empty, regretful, lonely, discouraged, and unfulfilled.

Procrastination is another deceptive tool of the devil. Good intentions do not bring us into the blessings of God — only obedience does. Our willful choice to obey God promptly is the lifeline between heart's desire and finished product.

Press on! Don't look back! Satan may think he is destroying you, but often he is giving you valuable experience that will keep you out of trouble.

Say This:

"No more deals. No more compromise and procrastination. Henceforth, I am walking in the will of God."

Integrity

The integrity of the upright shall guide them, but the willful contrariness and crookedness of the treacherous shall destroy them. — PROVERBS 11:3

Our society has gradually declined over the past years to the place that it no longer honors God. We live in a world that is not concerned about integrity. Often, the world is more concerned about quantity than quality. People carelessly speak half-truths and exaggerations, making deceptive comments that lead many to believe something that is not true.

As believers, we are in the world but not of the world. (John 17:11,14.) Let's not act like the world.

Let's do an integrity check. What does the word *integrity* mean? It is a "firm adherence to a code or standard of values."[1] Our standard should be much higher than the world's. There are certain things we wouldn't even think of doing, but there are too many compromises, even in the lives of God's people. There are things we do that Jesus would not do, and He is our standard of integrity.

If we want to enjoy prosperity, we must walk in integrity. Integrity is being committed to a life of excellence, as our God is excellent.

Integrity is keeping our word. Commitment is giving our all and finishing what we start.

Keep your word, even if it costs you. Be committed to integrity.

Do This:

Count the cost before saying you will do something. Think it over; will you see it through to the finish? Be a person of integrity.

Confidence

*Not that we are fit (qualified and sufficient in ability)
of ourselves..., but our power and ability and sufficiency
are from God.* — 2 CORINTHIANS 3:5

No matter how qualified and able we may be,
without confidence we won't accomplish much.

What is *confidence?* Webster says it is "trust or
faith."[1] *Confidence* also means "a feeling of assurance,
especially of self-assurance," "security," "self-confidence."[1] *Self-confidence* is the belief, "I'm acceptable
and able."

Jesus said, *...apart from Me...you can do nothing
(John 15:5).* That does not mean we are able to do
nothing at all; it means we are not able to do
anything worthwhile.

We need to come to a state of utter bankruptcy
in our own ability apart from Christ. It does not

matter what we can or cannot do. Without God, we are helpless; with Him nothing is impossible to us. (Matthew 19:26.)

There are two main reasons that we are not used by God for greater things: (1) we think we are something in ourselves, or (2) we don't know who we are in Christ.

We try to accomplish things in the flesh, not realizing that without God we are powerless. But if God is with us, our natural deficiencies don't matter. We are ...*self-sufficient in Christ's sufficiency (Philippians 4:13).*

Whatever you need to do, you can do it because of Christ in you.

Do This:

Remember the Lord sees your heart. Be confident in His love for you. Know that you are accepted and you are able through Christ.

Confidence in Prayer

And this is the confidence (the assurance, the privilege of boldness) which we have in Him: [we are sure] that if we ask anything (make any request) according to His will..., He listens to and hears us. — 1 JOHN 5:14

We are to walk in confidence in every area. Prayer is one of the ways we can show that our confidence is in God. If we pray about things instead of worrying and trying to work them out ourselves, we say by our actions, "Lord, I trust You in this situation."

I believe many of us pray and then wonder if God heard. We wonder if we prayed properly or long enough. We wonder if we used the right phrases, enough Scripture, etc. We cannot pray properly with doubt and unbelief. We must pray with faith.

God has been encouraging me to realize that simple faith-filled prayer gets the job done. I don't have to repeat things over and over. He hears me the first time. I don't need to get fancy in my wording. I can just be me and know that He hears me and understands.

We should simply present our request and believe that God has heard us and will answer at the right time.

Have confidence in your prayers. Believe God hears even simple, childlike prayer coming from a sincere heart.

Pray This:

"Father, I thank You that You hear me when I pray. I believe I have the petitions I request of You. In Jesus' name, amen."

Put No Confidence in the Flesh

...and put no confidence or dependence [on what we are] in the flesh and on outward privileges and physical advantages and external appearances. — PHILIPPIANS 3:3

As the children of God, we have the privilege of trusting God for everything — not just some things — but everything! When we trust, we are joyful, peaceful, and free of pressure. On the other hand, when our confidence is in ourselves, we struggle and usually fail.

We need to set a goal for ourselves: to put no confidence in the flesh.

It requires determined effort not to trust in ourselves. It seems the "natural" flow of the flesh to trust in itself. Galatians teaches us that the flesh is opposed to the Spirit, and the Spirit is opposed to the flesh. (Galatians 5:17.) If we sow to the flesh, we will reap destruction. (Galatians 6:8.)

Our confidence (trust) belongs to us, and we must choose where and in whom to place it. We know that Jesus is the Rock — everything else is like sinking sand. That means we are wise when we place our trust in Him — the only true source of stability.

Seek to grow to the place where you can honestly say, "In Christ alone I place my trust." Then and only then comes the joy, the peace, the victory — and He gets all the glory.

Pray This:

"Father, I place my trust and confidence in You. I surrender my will to You and receive Your joy and peace. In Jesus' name, amen."

Growing Up Without Giving Up

Rather, let our lives lovingly express truth [in all things, speaking truly, dealing truly, living truly]. Enfolded in love, let us grow up in every way and in all things into Him Who is the Head, [even] Christ (the Messiah, the Anointed One). — EPHESIANS 4:15

Growing up spiritually is not always easy. It might be said that we believers have to endure many "growing pains." Due to the challenging times, often we are tempted to give up. We all need to realize the progress we have made.

Perhaps you have been struggling with yourself. You know that you need to change. You desire to be like Jesus. And yet you feel that you are making no progress. The first thing you must realize is that you *are* making progress. Little by little, you are changing.

Take some time and think about where you were when you first accepted Christ into your heart. Listen to the Holy Spirit instead of listening to the devil! The way to listen to the Holy Spirit is by following your heart — not your head or your feelings. Learn to live beyond your feelings.

Don't compare yourself with other people. Everyone has strengths and weaknesses. Be patient with yourself. Keep pressing on and believe that you are changing every day.

Don't give up! You are growing up!

Say This:

"Christ is my life. I grow up into Him Who is the Head. Through Him I have joy unspeakable and full of glory!" (1 Peter 1:8 KJV.)

Get Started and Never Quit

I press on toward the goal to win the [supreme and heavenly] prize to which God in Christ Jesus is calling us upward. — PHILIPPIANS 3:14

Has God told you to do something and you intend to obey Him at some time, but you just have not gotten around to it yet? Good intentions are not obedience. You have not obeyed until you have taken the action that God instructed you to take.

I encourage you to get started moving in the right direction. Begin to pray about your vision. If you do not have one, pray for one, and in the meantime, become associated with somebody who does have one. Get around a visionary and you may become one.

Get started moving in a positive direction. Speak positive things about yourself and your life; believe that God can use you.

Get excited! It feels better than being bored. If God has given you a vision, you must be committed to bringing that vision to pass under the leadership of the Holy Spirit. Establish short-term and long-term goals, then move toward those goals daily in prayer and in action.

Visions do not come to pass overnight, so you must be patient and just keep moving even if you do not see any visual evidence of success for a long time.

Get started and never quit!

Do This:

Start moving in a positive direction. Take steps of obedience. Don't just have good intentions. Be a doer of the Word.

Holy Determination

I have fought the good (worthy, honorable, and noble) fight, I have finished the race, I have kept (firmly held) the faith. — 2 TIMOTHY 4:7

I believe that the Spirit of God fills us with holy determination. It is something that God has in Him and imparts to us through His Spirit. We are not to be quitters or the type of people who are easily defeated.

We must be determined to overcome the past; to go forward and not be stagnant.

We must not be afraid of difficulty. Things worth having never come easy. The definition of *determination* is: "The act of making or arriving at a decision.... The quality of being resolute or firm in purpose."[1] We must be decisive and stick to our decisions.

If you find yourself being double-minded about something, I encourage you to ask yourself what you believe God placed in your heart in the beginning; then stick with that. Don't head in another direction now due to weariness.

I believe you have what it takes to live in victory. If you have accepted Jesus as your Lord and Savior, His determination lives in you because He lives in you.

Fight the good fight of faith. Run the race to win. Be determined to take the prize. Don't give up and don't give in.

You can make it!

Do This:

Depend on God's strength — not your own. Say aloud several times every day, "I will never give up! I will finish the race!"

The Power of Patience

For you have need of steadfast patience and endurance, so that you may perform and fully accomplish the will of God, and thus receive and carry away [and enjoy to the full] what is promised. — HEBREWS 10:36

The Word of God promises that the patient man will be perfect and entire, lacking nothing. (James 1:4 KJV.) A patient man is a powerful man. He can remain calm in the storm. He has control over his mouth. His thoughts remain loving in times when people's behavior becomes challenging.

Without patience we cannot endure to see the fulfillment of our faith. Everything does not come to us immediately upon believing. There is a waiting period involved in receiving from God. It is during that period that our faith is tested and purified. Only if we endure and wait patiently will we experience the joy of seeing what we have believed for.

Patience is not only the ability to wait, but also the ability to keep a good attitude while waiting. Waiting is a part of life that cannot be avoided. We will spend a great deal of our lives waiting; if we don't learn to do it well (patiently), we will be quite miserable. God is so patient with us. And we are to imitate Him.

Be encouraged to actively pursue patience – it will lead you into God's power.

Pray This:

"Lord, help me to exercise every kind of endurance and patience, perseverance, and forbearance with joy (Colossians 1:11). In Jesus' name, amen."

You Can Triumph in the Midst of Your Trials!

And after you have suffered a little while, the God of all grace..., Who has called you to His [own] eternal glory in Christ Jesus, will Himself complete and make you what you ought to be, establish and ground you securely, and strengthen, and settle you. — 1 PETER 5:10

In John 16:33 Jesus tells us that in the world we will have tribulation. Trials and tribulations seem to be a part of life. We should learn how to triumph in the midst of them.

Trials can make us bitter or better. The devil hopes to steal our faith and leave us bitter and angry at God.

God intends to strengthen our faith, purify it so it comes forth like gold, develop patience in us, and give us experience that will help others. (1 Peter 1:5-7.)

We are taught to endure patiently. (1 Peter 2:20.) To endure is to outlast the problem. Patience is a fruit of the Spirit. (Galatians 5:22.) It is not just waiting, it is how we act while we are waiting.

To triumph in trials we must learn stability — remain the same, continue in our commitments, and walk in love. Going through hard times and continuing to be good and kind to others is a sure way to triumph in trials.

If you are in a time of trials, they don't have to defeat you — let them make you stronger.

Say This:

"I will triumph in the midst of my trials by remaining stable. I will continue to walk in love and the fruit of the Spirit."

Going All the Way Through With God

When you pass through the waters, I will be with you, and through the rivers, they will not overwhelm you. When you walk through the fire, you will not be burned or scorched.... — ISAIAH 43:2

God wants us to be diligent and go all the way through with Him, not just go until the way becomes difficult, and then stop there. One of our greatest challenges is to face our mountains rather than trying to go around them.

Sometimes we go around and around the same mountain, and we end up like the Israelites in the wilderness who wandered around for forty years. (Deuteronomy 2:1-3.) We must learn to face our mountains, determined to go all the way through with God. That is the only path to victory.

I encourage you to go all the way through with God no matter how difficult it may seem. Let God have His way in your life. Pray for God's will and not your own will. God's way is for you to set your face like flint, dig in both heels, and go all the way through.

By the way, the attitude that you have while you are going through is most important. The Word says that it is to be a joyful attitude, otherwise you may have to make the trip again. (James 1:2-4.)

Pray This:

"Father, thank You for infusing me with inner strength so that I am ready for and equal to anything. (Philippians 4:13.) In Jesus' name, amen."

Spiritual Warfare

*For we are not wrestling with flesh and blood
[contending only with physical opponents], but against...
the spirit forces of wickedness in the heavenly (supernatural) sphere.* — EPHESIANS 6:12

The attacks of Satan against the Church are of a
different nature than those in the past days — different in that they are more intense than ever before.
The enemy will not continuously use the same tactics
over and over, because once his method of attack is
discovered, it is no longer effective.

More people than ever are experiencing tremendous attacks against their minds. Many of God's
people are being attacked with sickness. Some of
them are experiencing great financial trauma. People
are enduring great attacks of fear.

How can you fight the devil who is the source of these attacks?

1. Praise is one way. Praise is a garment that will protect you from defeat. Put on the garment of praise.

2. Abiding in Christ and fellowshipping with Him is one of the best ways of engaging in spiritual warfare. Hide yourself in God, and His presence will protect you.

3. The Word of God is a two-edged sword. Your mind is the battlefield. When Satan says something to you, speak the Word back.

4. Walking in love is another form of spiritual warfare. Love gives: it is impossible to defeat Satan while leading a selfish lifestyle.

Use your spiritual weapons!

Do This:

Praise the Lord. Speak the Word of God. Abide in Christ. Walk in love. Use these weapons and begin to fight in a new way.

Battlefield of the Mind

...we lead every thought and purpose away captive into the obedience of Christ (the Messiah, the Anointed One). — 2 CORINTHIANS 10:5

According to 2 Corinthians 10:3-5, the mind is the battlefield. We are in a war, but it is a spiritual war that must be fought spiritually with spiritual weapons.

Using our spiritual weapons, we refute the enemy's lies, arguments, theories, reasonings, and every other thing that tries to exalt itself against the truth of God's Word.

We must take our thoughts captive and not indulge in the fleshly luxury of receiving and meditating on every thought that falls into our heads. We must exercise ourselves to "think about what we are thinking about." This takes some discipline and practice.

The primary weapon with which we do battle is the Word of God used in various ways — preached, taught, sung, confessed, meditated upon, written, and read. The Word of God has a cleansing effect on our minds and lives any way we use it.

I once had a negative, wandering, wondering mind. Now, after years of applying the Word of God and a lot of help from the Holy Spirit, I can say with confidence, "I have the mind of Christ." (1 Corinthians 2:16.)

You can win the battle in your mind — every stronghold can be torn down and every deception uncovered. Don't settle for anything less than complete freedom!

Say This:

"Thank You, Lord, for Your Word that renews my mind and sets me free. I have the mind of Christ! In Jesus' name, amen."

The Battle Belongs to the Lord

...Be not afraid or dismayed at this great multitude; for the battle is not yours, but God's. — 2 CHRONICLES 20:15

Are you struggling with issues in your life, and frustrated because you never get a breakthrough no matter what you do? You will never win if you are fighting your own battles.

God never loses a battle. He has a definite battle plan — and when we follow it, we always win.

Perhaps you are in a circumstance right now and you need to hear God say, "The battle is not yours, but Mine!"

Worship is a battle position! As we worship God for Who He is and for His attributes, those attributes are released in our lives.

Worship God for His ability and might, and you will see them released on your behalf.

Try bowing down a few times a day and giving thanks. Just be sure your heart is in what you are doing. Working formulas or entering into "dead works" never produces anything of value.

I am sure your heart frequently fills up with love and worship for God. If you are not already doing so, take an extra step and add some outward action to your heart attitude.

Follow God's battle plan. It is enjoyable, unique, and effective. Praise and worship confuse the enemy. Take your position, and you will see the enemy's defeat.

Do This:

Bow before God and thank Him for His goodness and mercy. Worship Him for Who He is, not just for what you need from Him.

You Can Be the Victor Instead of the Victim

Yet amid all these things we are more than conquerors and gain a surpassing victory through Him Who loved us. — ROMANS 8:37

Are you hurting — physically, emotionally, or mentally? Did you know that you can increase or decrease the intensity of your pain by the way you handle it?

I know from experience and the Word of God that it is possible to be the victor instead of the victim.

The key thing to see is that the victory is "through Christ." If you and I can learn how to lean on God and receive from Him whatever we need, we truly can do all things through Christ Who strengthens us. (Philippians 4:13.)

God is more than enough for any situation. He has promised to enable us and to be our helper. As we come into close fellowship with Him — spending time with Him and talking with Him in a simple, familiar way — we begin to draw strength from Him.

The number one thing I learned was that I had to lean on the Lord to strengthen me. The second thing I learned was not to talk about the problem or even to think about it unless absolutely necessary.

Whatever you may be going through right now, keep your eyes and your conversation on the Lord and off your situation.

Remember — this too shall pass.

Do This:

Submit yourself to God in all things. Spend quality time with Him. Wait in His presence, and you will find He is more than enough.

Behold, I Give You Power

Behold! I have given you authority and power to trample upon serpents and scorpions, and [physical and mental strength and ability] over all the power that the enemy [possesses]; and nothing shall in any way harm you. — LUKE 10:19

Far too many believers are fainthearted, weak in determination, and diseased with an "I can't" attitude — they are lacking in power.

You and I don't have to beg God to give us power. We just need to realize and accept that we have been given power and then walk in what is already ours. We must develop and maintain a "power consciousness" — an aggressive, power-packed attitude.

God has given us spiritual power for spiritual warfare. Spiritual power is released when our faith is firm. When we walk in faith we can approach every situation with an attitude of enemy-conquering faith.

An attitude of confidence will exude from us when we know who we are in Christ and believe in the power that the Bible says is ours through faith.

Do you desire to be a powerful believer? Try approaching every situation in your life (no matter how large or small) with a simple, childlike faith — believing that God is good, that He has a good plan for your life, and that He is working in your situation.

You have power. Walk in it!

Say This:

"The Greater One lives in me. I am full of God's miracle-working power. I am going to walk in what is mine."

Get Thee Behind Me, Satan!

Submit yourselves therefore to God. Resist the devil, and he will flee from you. — JAMES 4:7 KJV

As believers living under the New Covenant, we are taught that we have authority over Satan and demonic spirits. (Luke 10:19.) Resisting the devil at his onset is vital to victory over the enemy. (1 Peter 5:8,9.)

The Bible teaches us how we can have dominion over the works of darkness. We can learn how to open the windows of heaven and close the gates of hell.

The mouth is either a door to blessing or to trouble. We may open a few wrong doors with our mouth; we should learn how to close them quickly.

Repentance and application of the blood of Jesus by faith is the way to close doors that have been opened to Satan such as the doors of strife, anger, and unforgiveness. We must be quick to forgive; offense and strife are not emotional luxuries we can afford.

The door of compromise is Satan's favorite entrance by which to gradually draw us into a web of sin that is devastating for us in the end.

The Bible teaches us the importance of keeping a tender and clean conscience. Without proper respect for the conscience, we will never enjoy authority over the devil.

Remember: Knowing what to do will not do you any good unless you do it!

Do This:

Master sin by doing the Word on a daily basis. Obey the promptings of the Spirit and keep a clear conscience.

Learn To Enforce the Defeat of the Devil

My people are destroyed for lack of knowledge....
— HOSEA 4:6

A growing interest in the supernatural in these last days makes it more important than ever that we become knowledgeable about key truths in order to avoid the pitfalls of deception. Everything that looks good isn't God; everything that is supernatural isn't spiritual.

This is no time for us believers to have our heads stuck in the sand.

First, we must realize that the devil, demons, and evil spirits are real. (1 Peter 5:8.)

Second, we must recognize Satan's tactics and know his vulnerable points as well as he knows ours, so we can counterattack him. (2 Corinthians 2:11.)

Third, we need to have knowledge of and exercise our God-given authority. (Luke 10:19.) We have authority and power to walk all over the devil! Satan has no right to do anything to us unjustly. We can protect ourselves with knowledge of God's Word.

This is a very important day and hour in which we are living. Only when we determine to seek the truth — from God's Word, through anointed teachers and preachers, and in our own personal study and prayer time — will we know how to successfully overcome the deception of the enemy and help others do the same.

Know your enemy! Enforce his defeat! You can fight the devil and win!

Pray This:

"Father, thank You for giving me authority over all the power that the enemy possesses so that he cannot harm me. In Jesus' name, amen."

Are You Wearing Your Armor or Carrying It?

Put on God's whole armor [the armor of a heavy-armed soldier which God supplies], that you may be able successfully to stand up against [all] the strategies and the deceits of the devil. — EPHESIANS 6:11

God supplies us with what we need to walk in victory. He supplies us with the armor and instructs us to put it on. We are to wear it, not carry it!

Many believers are carrying their armor instead of wearing it. God-inspired action is essential to victorious living.

Weak-willed, weak-minded believers are no threat to the devil. God desires that we possess the land. It will never happen unless we know the importance of staying strong in the Lord and in the power of His might.

We must be determined to finish our course and not give up. God-inspired, God-directed action is the key to victory. Too many people attempt to stand in their own strength, and they always fail.

Strength comes from spending time with God and purposely drawing from Him. Trusting God and praying are vital power sources.

When we wait in God's presence, there is a divine exchange. We exchange our nothingness for His everything. Our weakness is swallowed up in His strength.

Be strong in the Lord. Put on the whole armor of God. Don't carry it — wear it!

Say This:

"I am a believer. I walk in faith. God's strength is in me so that I always overcome. I am more than a conqueror."

The Word, the Name, the Blood

For the weapons of our warfare are not physical [weapons of flesh and blood], but they are mighty before God for the overthrow and destruction of strongholds. —
2 CORINTHIANS 10:4

The closer we approach the Second Coming of Jesus, the more fiercely Satan attacks. He seeks to defeat the corporate Church and its individual members.

There is no hope of defeating the devil without a revelation concerning the power of the Word, the name, and the blood of Christ.

The Word of God is not only a defensive weapon, but also an offensive one. As we speak the Word out of our mouths in faith, we wield a mighty two-edged sword that destroys the enemy.

Jesus gave us the power of attorney to use His name. The believer who truly has faith in the power of Jesus' name — and uses the name — will do great harm to the kingdom of darkness.

The blood is also a powerful weapon. We use our mouths in prayer to put the blood by faith on whatever needs protection.

God's grace showers blessings on us as we pray according to the Word, in the name, depending on the shed blood.

The Word, the name, and the blood are at the top of the list of those simple, but powerful, tools given to the Church to thoroughly defeat Satan.

Use your spiritual weapons!

Pray This:

"Father, thank You for giving me Your Word, Your name, and Your blood so that I am not weak and defenseless against the devil."

Who Is in Control?

But I say, walk and live [habitually] in the [Holy] Spirit [responsive to and controlled and guided by the Spirit].... — GALATIANS 5:16

Who is in control of your life? Is it you or is it God?

We are to willingly give the Holy Spirit control of our lives, allowing Him to lead and guide us. Most of us would say this is the desire of our heart, but precious few of us are doing it. What is the problem?

Our flesh tries to control. Galatians says plainly that the flesh is continually opposed to the Spirit. (Galatians 5:17.) What the flesh wants, the Spirit never wants. And what the Spirit desires, the flesh never agrees with.

We must refuse the evil and choose the good. The Holy Spirit's role in our lives includes prompting us to make correct choices, but His role is not — and never will be — to force us to make them.

God will never hurt us. He wants us to trust His direction enough simply to obey it, even if we don't totally understand it. When we willingly give the Holy Spirit control of our daily lives, He leads us into victory.

Give the Holy Spirit control of your life. He will lead you into the perfect will of God for you, which includes exceeding, abundant blessings, peace, and joy.

Do This:

Take inventory of all the things that try to control you and begin resisting everything except the control of the Holy Spirit.

How Can I Be Holy?

For it is written, You shall be holy, for I am holy.
— 1 PETER 1:16

Anyone who truly loves God wants to be holy. We desire to be like Him, and He is holy. Holiness signifies separation unto God. A state of holiness results in conduct befitting those so separated.

The Lord instructs us to do certain things, but He also provides us the ability to do what He requires. We struggle and labor when we try to do what He wants in our own strength, instead of calling upon His strength by faith.

The seed of holiness is planted in us at the New Birth. As we work with the Holy Spirit and water that seed with God's Word and our obedience, we begin to see positive changes in our behavior and in all other areas of life.

Many Christians spend most of their lives waiting to see themselves change before they will believe anything positive about themselves. But the good news is that God sees our hearts. We have a desire to do what is right because He has given us a new heart and put His Spirit within us.

When we start believing what the Word says about us more than what we see or do, then our behavior begins to radically and rapidly change.

Believe it: You are holy, because God says so!

Pray This:

"Father, thank You for making me holy by Your mercy and grace, and by the sacrifice and bloodshed of Your Son. In Jesus' name, amen."

The Wonderful Holy Spirit

And I will ask the Father, and He will give you another Comforter (Counselor, Helper, Intercessor, Advocate, Strengthener, and Standby), that He may remain with you forever. — JOHN 14:16

We serve a Triune God: Father, Son, and Holy Spirit — one God, three persons.

The Holy Spirit is the One Who makes us holy. The Father willed it, the Son paid for it, and the Holy Spirit does it. We become the sanctuary of God because of the presence of the Holy One in us. The Holy Spirit is the agent in the process of sanctification that accomplishes what needs to be wrought in us.

It is vital that we understand the ministry of the Holy Spirit so we can appreciate it and cooperate with it.

It is the Holy Spirit Who prompts us to pray and Who teaches us how to pray. He strengthens us in our time of need. He alone can minister to our inner man where comfort and refreshing are so often needed as we live out our lives here on the earth.

The Holy Spirit must be allowed to be in charge. We cannot change the things in our life that need to be changed, but the Holy Spirit can.

Trust the Holy Spirit. Begin today to benefit from His ministry. Let Him show you new ways to approach old problems.

Say This:

"The Holy Spirit lives in me. He is my Comforter, my Counselor, my Helper, my Intercessor, my Advocate, my Strengthener, and my Standby!"

Have You Been in the Wilderness Long Enough?

The Lord our God said to us in Horeb, You have dwelt long enough on this mountain. Turn and take up your journey.... — DEUTERONOMY 1:6,7

As long as we have wilderness attitudes, we will continue living in the wilderness. Jesus died so we could live in the Promised Land — the land of abundance.

It was only an eleven-day journey to the Promised Land, yet the Israelites wandered in the wilderness for forty years murmuring, grumbling, complaining, and blaming Moses and God for their troubles.

(Deuteronomy 1:1-7). Their lack of progress was due to their attitude.

Having a good attitude in a trying situation is at least 90 percent of the battle. We can win over anything as long as we have a godly attitude. There will always be trials in life, but as we trust God and continue doing what He shows us to do, we always come out victorious.

Don't be afraid to walk in the light. As God brings your faults into the light to expose and remove them, it may be uncomfortable. This kind of discomfort, however, is temporary.

God loves you very much, and He has an excellent plan for your life. Follow the Holy Spirit, and He will lead you swiftly through the wilderness into the Promised Land.

Take the shortcut through the wilderness — don't go the long way around!

Do This:

Ask the Holy Spirit to start convicting you of any wrong attitudes that are not pleasing to God so that with His help you can change them immediately.

Beware of Self-Exaltation

Therefore humble yourselves [demote, lower your-selves in your own estimation] under the mighty hand of God, that in due time He may exalt you. — 1 PETER 5:6

We are not to promote ourselves. True promotion comes from God. (Psalm 75:6,7.)

I can promote myself but from experience I have discovered that if I put myself somewhere, I have to struggle to keep myself there. If I wait for God to put me in a position, He also keeps me.

It takes patience to wait on God's promotion, but waiting on Him honors Him — and the person who honors God will be honored by God. (1 Samuel 2:30.) It is yet to be seen what the Lord can do through a man or woman who will give Him all the glory.

We must learn to allow God to take the lead role in our daily life and future. How much we are depending upon Him is clearly seen by how willing we are to wait on Him for what we want.

Trusting God does not mean that we do nothing. It does, however, mean that we do *only* what God leads us to do.

God can use only the humble. The degree of humility in which we walk determines how much God is able to use us.

Wait on the Lord! (Psalm 27:14.) His way is better. His timing is perfect.

Do This:

Allow God to take the lead role in your life. Wait on Him, and everything will turn out better in the end.

Walk in the Spirit

But I say, walk and live [habitually] in the [Holy] Spirit [responsive to and controlled and guided by the Spirit]; then you will certainly not gratify the cravings and desires of the flesh (of human nature without God).
— GALATIANS 5:16

There is a price to be paid in order to walk in the Spirit. We must say no to some things to which we would rather say yes, and say yes to some things to which we would rather say no. We must follow the prompting (leading, guiding, and working) of the Holy Spirit through our own spirit.

To walk in the Spirit, we must stay filled with the Spirit. This is accomplished by continually choosing right thoughts, conversation, companionship, music, entertainment, etc.

To do God's will, we must be ready to suffer. If our flesh desires to walk one way and God's Spirit leads in another, a willful decision to be obedient will provoke suffering in the flesh.

The good news is, if we choose to walk in the Spirit daily, we will die to self-centeredness and gain freedom to serve God. We will experience righteousness, peace, and joy in the Holy Spirit. We will live in victory no matter what comes against us.

Invest now for your future: Walk in the Spirit. Start making right choices. Be persistent — and expect to be blessed.

Do This:

Determine to say yes when the Spirit says yes, and no when the Spirit says no. Crucify your flesh and walk in the Spirit.

The Fruit of the Spirit

But the fruit of the [Holy] Spirit...is love, joy (gladness), peace, patience (an even temper, forbearance), kindness, goodness (benevolence), faithfulness, gentleness (meekness, humility), self-control (self-restraint, continence).... — GALATIANS 5:22,23

Each one of us is presented with a variety of opportunities to manifest the fruit of the Spirit every day of our lives. The fruit of the Spirit operating in our lives is linked to our spiritual maturity. God has shown me that the fruit should be the container in which the glorious gifts of the Spirit are carried.

There is a responsibility attached to Christianity to walk in integrity — to "walk the walk," even when nobody notices.

196

At some time in life we may find ourselves involved in a relationship with someone who is difficult. We may try our best to be sweet — to obey God and bear the fruit of the Spirit despite the way the other person acts. We must not become discouraged; we must "keep on keeping on." Some of the most severe tests in our lives can involve relationships that try the very fruit in which we are attempting to walk.

Learn to operate in the fruit of the Spirit. God has a good plan for you. The manifestation of the fruit of His Spirit through you makes the difference in how soon you begin walking in that glorious plan.

Say This:

"I allow the fruit of the Spirit to manifest in my life so that I may walk in the glorious plan God has for me."

Righteousness, Peace, and Joy in the Holy Spirit

[After all] the kingdom of God is not a matter of [getting the] food and drink [one likes], but instead it is righteousness (that state which makes a person acceptable to God) and [heart] peace and joy in the Holy Spirit.

— ROMANS 14:17

God's Kingdom is not made up of worldly things but consists of something far greater and more beneficial. God does bless us with material things, but the Kingdom is much more than that: It is righteousness, peace, and joy in the Holy Spirit.

Righteousness is not the result of what we do, but rather what Jesus has done for us. (1 Corinthians 1:30) When we accept this truth by faith and receive it personally, a great burden is lifted from us.

Peace is so wonderful — it is definitely Kingdom living. We are to pursue peace, crave it, and go after it. (Psalm 34:14; 1 Peter 3:11.) Jesus is our peace. (Ephesians 2:14.) God's will for you and me is the peace that passes all understanding. (Philippians 4:7 KJV.)

Joy can be anything from calm delight to extreme hilarity. Joy improves our countenance, our health, and the quality of our lives. It strengthens our witness to others and makes some of the less desirable circumstances in life more bearable.

It is clear in the Word of God: Seek God and His Kingdom, and He will take care of everything else. (Matthew 6:33.)

Say This:

"I seek first the Kingdom of God. I seek righteousness, peace, and joy in the Holy Spirit. All other things are added unto me."

The Ruling Power of Love

Above all things have intense and unfailing love for one another, for love covers a multitude of sins [forgives and disregards the offenses of others]. — 1 PETER 4:8

It is not at all natural to the carnal man to walk in love toward others when he is undergoing personal trials. The believer, however, is equipped with the power of the Holy Spirit to enable him to do just that.

It is God's will for us to rule in the midst of our enemies. If God removes every hindrance, we never stretch and grow. There are many aspects to ruling over the enemy, but the ruling power of love has been one of the most amazing to me.

I believe walking in love protects us. It is spiritual warfare. We must employ every effort in the power of God's grace to maintain a fervent love walk.

Let us concentrate on our love walk, study love, and make an effort to show love to others. It is more than talk or theory — it is action. Our flesh may not always feel like loving others, but if we want to rule over the enemy, we must say, "It is no longer I who live, but Christ Who lives in me." (Galatians 2:20.)

You have Holy Ghost power to do what you know is right — not just what you feel like doing.

Say This:

"I rule over the devil by resisting him and walking in the love of God in every situation and under all circumstances."

The Power of Words

Let the words of my mouth and the meditation of my heart be acceptable in Your sight, O Lord, my [firm, impenetrable] Rock and my Redeemer. — PSALM 19:14

Words are containers for power. They carry creative or destructive power. They can tear down or build up. They can encourage or discourage. It is not acceptable to God when we use our mouths to bring hurt and destruction.

Properly chosen words can change our life. Just think of it, we can use our mouths and the power of words to heal relationships or to destroy them.

Right words can affect our future in a positive way. We can find out what the Word of God has to say about God's promises and what is available to us as believers; then we can prophesy our future. We can begin to "call those things that be not as though they were." (Romans 4:17 KJV.) We can take faith-filled words and reach out into the spiritual realm and begin to pull from God's storehouse the manifestation of those things that He has promised.

There are right and wrong uses of the mouth. Our mouths should belong to the Lord, and we should discipline what comes out of them. We should speak His words and use our mouths for His purpose.

Determine to use your mouth to bring encouragement not discouragement.

Pray This:

"Lord, let the words of my mouth and the meditation of my heart be acceptable in Your sight. In Jesus' name, amen."

Marriage: Triumph or Tragedy?

Wives, understand and support your husbands....
Husbands, go all out in your love for your wives....
— EPHESIANS 5:22,25 MESSAGE

There is nothing more wonderful than a great marriage — and nothing more miserable than a bad one. Plenty of marriages fall into both categories, but even more are in an "in-between" category: They are just mediocre.

Why? Could it be because they have gone so long without any marital maintenance that everything in them is in need of repair?

My husband and I are very much in love, and we have a great marriage. However, we have learned that to keep it great, we must pay regular attention to it.

God has helped us to learn that anything that is not growing is dying.

Keep freshness in your marriage. Have fun. Laugh together, work hard together, but don't forget to play together. A proper balance must be maintained or the adversary will get in and cause trouble.

Don't spend all of your time together talking about problems. Use wisdom. Don't confront explosive issues when either (or both) of you are tired or not feeling up to par.

Remember that love covers a multitude of sins. (1 Peter 4:8.) Little acts of kindness will nourish your love and help you be more willing to overlook each other's faults and weaknesses.

Do your part to have a great marriage!

Do This:

Confront mediocrity in your marriage. Do all you can do to make sure your marriage is a triumph and not a tragedy.

Children: A Big Blessing and a Big Responsibility

Train up a child in the way he should go [and in keeping with his individual gift or bent], and when he is old he will not depart from it. — PROVERBS 22:6

Children are a blessing from the Lord (Psalm 127:3), but they are also a big responsibility. It is very important that we understand that we are stewards of God's gifts and talents, not owners.

As stewards, we should seek understanding about God's will for our children and train them in that direction. Children must be taught right from wrong, loved unconditionally, and — as they grow up — given freedom to follow their own heart. We are to help our children be all they can be in Christ.

Right, godly correction is vital to proper child development. To correct a child in an unscriptural way is often worse than not to correct him at all.

As parents, our words have a dramatic, and often long-lasting effect on our children. Thus, we must be careful to use our words to build our children up and not to tear them down. We must pray that the Holy Spirit will help us train our children in a godly way — not the world's way — but God's way.

Remember, if you train your children right when they are young, you will reap good fruit later on.

Pray This:

"Father, give me understanding concerning Your will for my children so that I may train them in that direction. In Jesus' name, amen."

A Godly Home

To keep Satan from getting the advantage over us; for we are not ignorant of his wiles and intentions.
— 2 Corinthians 2:11

We must be alert and watchful for Satan's tactics. One of his prime targets today is the family. He is very busy trying to bring to pass divorce, marital problems, sibling rivalry, division between parents and children, and family strife.

A strong, godly family that walks in love is a major threat to the enemy. God's plan is agreement, harmony, and unity — a family joined together as one whose purpose is to do the will of the Father. Mercy needs to be abundant in our homes. Minor issues should be overlooked.

Allow Jesus to be the Head of every area of your home. Have some house rules that get everybody involved in keeping the home a place of peace. Here are some tips on peaceful living:

1. Speak in voice tones that bring peace. Avoid being harsh.
2. Build each other; don't tear down. Be positive.
3. Work together to keep order.
4. Have fun together on a regular basis. Laugh — it is like medicine.
5. Be merciful, freely forgiving because God has freely forgiven each of you.
6. Be slow to anger, slow to speak, and quick to hear.
7. Be slow to take offense.
8. Judge not.
9. Arrange your schedule so you don't have to hurry all the time.
10. Don't worry.

Pray This:

"Father, we desire to have a godly home. Therefore, we allow You to be Lord in every area of our lives. In Jesus' name, amen."

How To Succeed at Being Yourself

For we dare not make ourselves of the number, or compare ourselves with some that commend themselves: but they...comparing themselves among themselves, are not wise. — 2 Corinthians 10:12 kjv

People who don't accept themselves and get along with themselves have a difficult time accepting and getting along with other people.

If we don't like ourselves, we are not going to enjoy life very much. Once we have a revelation that God loves us unconditionally, we will be able to begin to accept ourselves and eventually produce good fruit in our relationship with others.

Stop for a while and ask yourself, "How do I feel about myself?"

I want to share ten tips on how to succeed at being yourself. I believe they will help you to develop more self-confidence and a better image of yourself as a child of God:

1. Never think or speak negatively about yourself.
2. Meditate on and speak positive things about yourself.
3. Never compare yourself with anyone else.
4. Focus on your potential not your limitations.
5. Find something you like to do and that you do well, then do it over and over.
6. Have the courage to be different. Be a God-pleaser, not a manpleaser.
7. Learn to cope with criticism.
8. Determine your own worth — don't let other people do it for you.
9. Keep your flaws in perspective.
10. Discover the true Source of confidence.

Do This:

Begin to see yourself as a child of God. Think and speak good things about yourself, knowing you are loved despite your weaknesses and flaws.

A Land of Abundance

But you shall [earnestly] remember the Lord your God, for it is He Who gives you power to get wealth, that He may establish His covenant which He swore to your fathers.... — DEUTERONOMY 8:18

God wants us to prosper. He wants people to see His goodness and how well He takes care of us. But we must desire God more than we desire His blessings. He tests us to make sure this is the case before He releases greater material blessings in our lives.

If God gives us more outward blessings than we have inner strength to handle, we never handle them in a way that brings glory to Him.

Perhaps you have been asking God for increase, and right now you are in the testing stage. Hold steady and continue to be thankful for what God has already done for you. Increase is coming!

God wants you to prosper radically — never doubt that. But He also wants you to be mature enough not to be led away from Him by material blessings.

Always remember to have a thankful heart for each of God's blessings. Express your thanksgiving to Him. A thankful heart shows maturity and establishes that you are ready for even more blessings. Never take for granted anything the Lord does for you.

Remember: God delights in the prosperity of His children. (Psalm 35:27.)

Do This:

Believe God for abundance and new levels of prosperity in every realm of your life. Also believe Him for new levels of maturity.

Celebrate Life

"The thief comes only to steal and kill and destroy; I have come that they may have life, and have it to the full." — JOHN 10:10 NIV

I am convinced that most people do not truly enjoy life. Unbelievers certainly don't, but it is very sad how many believers have not learned to really enjoy the life God has given them.

The Greek word for life is *zoe*, meaning the God-kind of life.[1] When an individual is born again, his spirit comes alive. He then needs to learn to enjoy that new life.

We need to learn how to celebrate life, to live it "to the full." We need to leave our problems in God's hands while we enjoy what is left.

Learn to be content no matter what your situation may be. Cast your care upon the Lord because He cares for you. (1 Peter 5:7.) Pray, tell God your need, and be thankful.

The passing of time brings change, restoration, and healing. Don't pass your life worrying, complaining, and being discontent. Everything and everybody changes. Nothing stays the same forever. Only Jesus never changes. (Hebrews 13:8.)

Dave and I always tell each other in rough times, "This too shall pass." If you remember that fact, you will be better able to be content and to have life "to the full."

Cultivate the habit of enjoying life.

Do This:

Celebrate life. It is a gift from God. Remember, the Bible says, *...whatever you do, do it all for the glory of God (1 Corinthians 10:31 NIV).*

How To Enjoy Everyday Life

Whatever may be your task, work at it heartily (from the soul), as [something done] for the Lord and not for men. — COLOSSIANS 3:23

In all of our lives there are large portions of our time that must be devoted to what may be called "common life and everyday business." We tend to see these chores as being quite different from the things we do that we consider to be holy. Most of us prefer the holy tasks over the common.

Seeing the two sides of our life as being in two entirely different categories usually causes quite a problem for us. Often we feel divided within ourselves struggling to get finished with "common life and everyday business" so we can return to "holy things," because we feel holier when we are engaged in what we believe to be holy.

Everything we do is to be offered to the Lord, and if it is done with a pure heart of love, it becomes holy. True liberty is the freedom not to have to live a divided life in which we categorize some things as common and some as holy.

The Lord is holy, and He lives in us, so that makes us holy. Therefore, wherever we go and whatever we do become holy if done unto Him.

Join me in this liberated lifestyle and begin to enjoy everyday life.

Say This:

"I am determined to enjoy every facet of my life: 'common life and everyday business' as well as my spiritual life."

Endnotes

In Christ

[1] *Webster's II New College Dictionary* (Boston/New York: Macmillan, 1996), s.v. "substitute."

[2] *Webster's II,* s.v. "identify."

Rested, Refreshed, Revived, Restored, Refilled

[1] *Webster's II,* s.v. "get."

[2] *Webster's II,* s.v. "receive."

The Spirit of Offense

[1] W.E. Vine, Merrill F. Unger, William White Jr., *Vine's Complete Expository Dictionary of Old and New Testament Words* (Nashville: Thomas Nelson, Inc., 1984), "New Testament Section," p. 441, s.v. "OFFENCE (OFFENSE)," A. Nouns.

Strife

[1] *Webster's II,* s.v. "get."

Be Anxious for Nothing

[1] Vine, "New Testament Section," p. 91, s.v. "CAST," A. Verbs, "to throw, hurl...."

The Search for Peace

[1] Vine, "New Testament Section," p. 558, s.v. "SEEK."

Seated in Heavenly Places

[1] *Webster's II,* s.v. "rest."

[2] Vine, "New Testament Section," pp. 1,2, s.v. "ABIDE, ABODE," A. Verbs.

Is God Dealing With You?

[1] Vine, "New Testament Section," p. 97, s.v. "CHASTEN, CHAS-

TENING, CHASTISE, CHASTISEMENT," A. Verb. "Primarily denotes 'to train children,'.... 'to chastise,' this being a part of the training, whether (a) by correcting with words, reproving, admonishing...."

Integrity

[1] *Webster's II,* s.v. "integrity."

Confidence

[1] *Webster's II,* s.v. "confidence."

Holy Determination

[1] *Webster's II,* s.v. "determination."

Celebrate Life

[1] Definition based on Vine, "New Testament Section," p. 367 s.v. "LIFE, LIVING, LIFETIME, LIFE-GIVING," A. Nouns. "Is used in the New Testament 'of life as a principle, life in the absolute sense, life as God has it, that which the Father has in Himself, and which He gave to the Incarnate Son to have in Himself...and which the Son manifested in the world....'"

About the Author

JOYCE MEYER has been teaching the Word of God since 1976 and in full-time ministry since 1980. She is the bestselling author of more than sixty inspirational books, including *In Pursuit of Peace*, *How to Hear from God*, *Knowing God Intimately*, and *Battlefield of the Mind*. She has also released thousands of teaching cassettes and a complete video library. Joyce's *Enjoying Everyday Life* radio and television programs are broadcast around the world, and she travels extensively conducting conferences. Joyce and her husband, Dave, are the parents of four grown children and make their home in St. Louis, Missouri.

To contact the author write:

Joyce Meyer Ministries
P. O. Box 655
Fenton, Missouri 63026
or call: (636) 349-0303
Internet Address: www.joycemeyer.org

Please include your testimony or help received from this book when you write. Your prayer requests are welcome.

To contact the author
in Canada, please write:
Joyce Meyer Ministries Canada, Inc.
Lambeth Box 1300
London, ON N6P 1T5
or call: (636) 349-0303

In Australia, please write:
Joyce Meyer Ministries-Australia
Locked Bag 77
Mansfield Delivery Centre
Queensland 4122
or call: 07 3349 1200

In England, please write:
Joyce Meyer Ministries
P. O. Box 1549
Windsor
SL4 1GT
Or call: (0) 1753-831102

Books by Joyce Meyer

Life in the Word Journal
Life in the Word Devotional
Be Anxious for Nothing
Be Anxious for Nothing Study Guide
Straight Talk Omnibus
Straight Talk on Loneliness
Straight Talk on Fear
Straight Talk on Insecurity
Straight Talk on Discouragement
Straight Talk on Worry
Straight Talk on Depression
Straight Talk on Stress
Don't Dread
Managing Your Emotions
Healing the Brokenhearted
Me and My Big Mouth!
Me and My Big Mouth! Study Guide
Prepare to Prosper
Do It Afraid!
Expect a Move of God in Your Life . . . Suddenly!
Enjoying Where You Are on the Way to Where You Are Going
The Most Important Decision You Will Ever Make
When, God, When?
Why, God, Why?
The Word, the Name, the Blood
Battlefield of the Mind
Battlefield of the Mind Study Guide
Tell Them I Love Them
Peace
The Root of Rejection
If Not for the Grace of God
If Not for the Grace of God Study Guide

JOYCE MEYER SPANISH TITLES
Las Siete Cosas Que Te Roban el Gozo
(Seven Things That Steal Your Joy)
Empezando Tu Día Bien (Starting Your Day Right)

BY DAVE MEYER
Life Lines